THE LUCY MAN

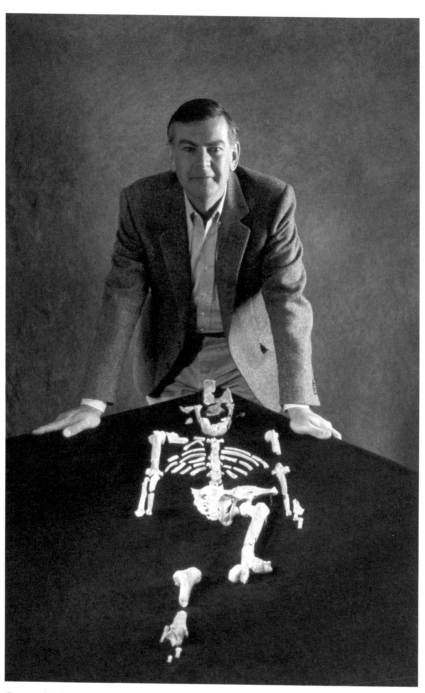

Don with Lucy.
(Courtesy of Nanci Kahn/Institute of Human Origins)

C A P Saucier

Foreword by
Donald C. Johanson

THE LUCY MAN

THE SCIENTIST WHO FOUND THE MOST FAMOUS FOSSIL
Ever!

PB Prometheus Books

59 John Glenn Drive
Amherst, New York 14228–2119

Published 2011 by Prometheus Books

Cover image of Dr. Donald C. Johanson with stone tool © 2011 Ferorelli
(Courtesy of Enrico Ferorelli)

Cover image of the comparison of the upper jaws of chimpanzee,
Australopithecus afarensis, and *Homo sapiens* © 2011 Kimbel/Institute of Human Origins
(Courtesy of William H. Kimbel/Institute of Human Origins)

Cover design by Nicole Sommer-Lecht

Inquiries should be addressed to
Prometheus Books
59 John Glenn Drive
Amherst, New York 14228-2119
VOICE: 716-691-0133
FAX: 716-691-0137
WWW.PROMETHEUSBOOKS.COM

15 14 13 12 11   5 4 3 2 1

Library of Congress Cataloging-in-Publication Data

Saucier, C.A.P., 1954–
    The Lucy man : the scientist who found the most famous fossil ever / by C.A.P. Saucier.
        p. cm.
    Includes bibliographical references and index.
    ISBN 978-1-61614-433-3 (pbk. : alk. paper)
    1. Johanson, Donald C. 2. Physical anthropologists—United States—Biography.
3. Physical anthropologists—Africa, East—Biography. 4. Lucy (Prehistoric hominid)
5. Australopithecus afarensis. 6. Fossil hominids—Africa, East. 7. Anthropology,
Prehistoric—Africa, East. I. Title.

GN50.6.J64S28 2011
599.9092—dc22
[B]   2010047441

531b

Printed in the United States of America on acid-free paper

Dedicated to all restless spirits
who search for truth.

But, in every age, one or two restless spirits, blessed with that constructive genius, which can only build on a secure foundation, or cursed with the mere spirit of scepticism, are unable to follow in the well-worn and comfortable track of their forefathers and contemporaries, and unmindful of thorns and stumbling blocks, strike out into paths of their own.

—Thomas H. Huxley, *Man's Place in Nature*

CONTENTS

Don in Land Rover. *(Courtesy of Angela Fisher)*

FOREWORD

I was only about eleven years old when I was first invited to look into a telescope pointed at Jupiter, the fifth planet from the sun. Named after the king of the Roman gods, Jupiter was the brightest object in the night sky, except of course when Venus appeared. My eyes focused on four small dots of light close to the banded planet itself. When I learned they were the same four moons that Galileo first observed in 1610, I was speechless.

Every night for a month, I looked at Jupiter at the same hour and saw how the moons changed position with respect to Jupiter. One night there were only three—where was the fourth moon? My friend kept asking me to figure it out, and finally I surmised that one of the rotating moons had gone behind Jupiter, and, with the use of astronomical tables, we calculated when it might reappear. What a thrill when within minutes of that projected time, the moon reemerged from the dark side of the planet.

Little did I realize that this was really my first science experiment. And by making observations and predictions, my curiosity had been rewarded and a passion for all things science was born. I had always harbored an interest in the world around me, and my earliest memory was as a two-year-old collecting newly born garden snakes and putting them into a tin can. The diversity of nature where I grew up in Hartford, Connecticut, was a continual source of inspiration—from feeding a squirrel that came to my bedroom window every morning to identifying trees, birds, insects, and so on. But the nights spent with Jupiter hooked me on science forever.

As a child I thought all science was fun, and the more I learned about something the more rewarded I felt. My thirst for science prompted me to get up at four in the morning and, with a hot cup of Ovaltine, huddle in the backyard on a cold mid-December night to watch the glorious Geminid meteor shower and record the number of meteors I had seen. Science was my favorite subject in school, and I quickly learned from a wonderful teacher how magical, how engaging, how cool it was to find a natural explanation for the universe around us.

I read whatever I could find on science, bought magazines, watched television shows, and built a chemistry lab in my basement. I saved money from doing chores and acquired a small microscope that opened a new kind of universe to me. I recall with particular vividness an experiment in elementary school that introduced me to the stunning observation that sometimes science can be stranger than fiction. We were doing experiments with water, one directed at understanding what elements made up water. An electrolysis experiment where a weak electrical current was passed through water and produced bubbles of gas at two tiny electrodes was mind-boggling. Two colorless gases began to collect in test tubes, displacing the water that had filled them.

My teacher, with some ceremony, carefully capped each test tube below the water so as to not lose the gas. He lit a small stick, blew it out, and (while it was still glowing) inserted it into one test tube—it burst into flame. Then he inserted the burning stick into the other test tube, and a small explosion occurred. He explained that the first test tube contained oxygen, which prompted the glowing ember to burn; and then, he explained, hydrogen—a dangerous explosive gas—prompted the small explosion in the other test tube. I was speechless. He was right: just as he had explained earlier, water—a liquid that we take for granted—is composed of two gases.

Throughout my life, science has been a source of never-ending fascination and reward, and it is the most objective way we have for understanding and finding meaningful explanations for the world around us. It shows us how the universe works (although that is still fervently debated), why life is so diverse, how our solar system is held together, and generally why things are the way they are. Pretty powerful stuff.

I encourage all young people to respect science and do their best to understand why it is so important for us. Take time to observe and question the things you see around yourself. Watch the moon change shape every night and build a model of the moon, the sun, and Earth to explain why that is the case. Use a flashlight and mimic a solar or lunar eclipse. Collect some pond water, peer through a microscope, and observe a magical world. Get your parents to buy you a chemistry set and have a home laboratory—but don't blow up the basement like I did!

For those of you who want to be scientists, develop a passion for something as soon as you can. When you are young, your mind is open, playful, curious, and questioning, and everything seems possible. Seize the opportunity to become engaged in science as soon as you feel the attraction, for it has been said that all great scientific breakthroughs happen before the age of thirty. James Watson, co–Nobel winner for the discovery of DNA, was just twenty-five years old when he made his breakthrough. Albert Einstein articulated his general theory of relativity when he was only thirty-two. I was thirty-one when I discovered the amazing fossil Lucy.

This book is more than the story of my life and my work finding Lucy. It is an up-to-date summary of the field of paleoanthropology—the science of how humans came to be, about which I care most deeply. Science for scientists and nonscientists alike gives us a sense of promise and reward. With some hard work we can all see the possibility of accomplishing great things. Only a few will win a Nobel Prize, but all of us who explore, question, or try to evaluate some natural phenomenon around us will live an enriched life that will make the world a better place for all humankind. Unlock that potential, your natural curiosity, and you will lead an enlightened life that will help you make informed choices about what is important in your life, such as your health, and develop an inquisitiveness that will enrich each and every day you walk planet Earth—or maybe even Mars.

Dr. Donald C. Johanson

CHAPTER One

A YOUNG SCIENTIST IN THE DESERT

As the young scientist walked through the Ethiopian desert, he carefully watched where he put his feet so he would not step on something other than the sand and the stones. He was hot and tired with the noontime sun bearing down on him, and he was about ready to stop looking and return to camp. "Just one more gully to explore," he thought as he pushed himself to continue.

In that gully, the young scientist found what he had spent years dreaming of—a fossilized arm bone of a long-extinct hominin. Hominins are our ancestors, near-human animals who walked upright on two feet. It was November 1974 and discovering this arm bone marked the beginning of Dr. Donald C. Johanson's distinguished career as a paleoanthropologist, a scientist who studies human origins and evolution.

After finding the arm bone, Don looked around expectantly for more bone pieces. He began to wonder if the leg bone, and the pieces of a pelvis, jaw, and skull he was collecting could

Don searching for fossils in the desert of Hadar, Ethiopia.
(Used by permission of David Brill)

belong to one individual. If so, who was this creature? Whoever this used to be, Don realized that finding so many pieces of one hominin skeleton was a major discovery. Up until that time, no fossil skeleton of a human ancestor had ever been found.

Don called to one of his colleagues to come see what he had discovered. His colleague Tom Gray rushed over to share Don's excitement. Both were hot, sweaty, and dirty, but they hugged each other and jumped up and down in jubilation.

Everyone back at camp was equally excited and spent the evening celebrating by listening to a tape of the Beatles that

Don holding a cast of Lucy's ulna (lower arm bone).
(Courtesy of the Institute of Human Origins)

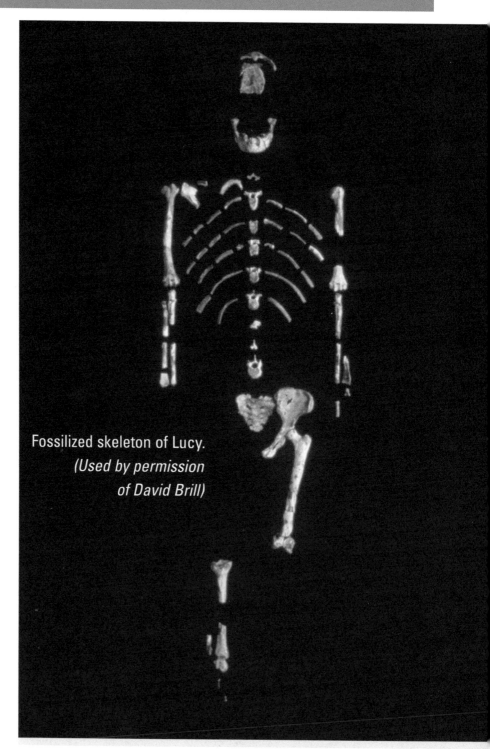

Fossilized skeleton of Lucy.
*(Used by permission
of David Brill)*

included the song "Lucy in the Sky with Diamonds." After observing that the bones were in proportion to one another and that there were no duplicates, Don determined that all the bones did indeed belong to one individual. By the small size of the bones and teeth and the shape of the pelvis (hip bones), he knew that it was female. The next morning, the fossil from the desert originally designated A.L. 288-1 had a name—Lucy.

WHY LUCY IS SPECIAL

What is it about one set of bones that makes it more important than another? Lucy's bones have been examined, measured, scanned, and studied by a variety of scientists for many years now. Her skeleton is special because it is so complete that it tells scientists a great deal about her as our ancestor. Lucy was different from any hominin discovered before her and therefore represented a new species. Her bones have been dated at 3.2 million years old (by potassium-argon analysis, described in chapter 4), which made her the oldest and best preserved skeleton of an upright-walking human ancestor ever found until the 1990s.

Lucy was a small creature who was about three and a half feet tall. From her wisdom teeth—the larger teeth in the back of the jaw that only erupt in mature hominins—Don knew she was fully grown when she died. Her bones were in remarkably good condition; they had not been chewed on by a predator, such as a hyena. Don is not sure how Lucy died. There is one small puncture wound in one of her pelvic bones. She may have been walking along the edge of an ancient lake or stream, getting a drink of water, or collecting turtle or crocodile eggs to eat when she was suddenly attacked by a crocodile and drawn into the water. Lucy's body settled into the mud, preventing a scavenger from pulling it apart and scattering her bones. Gradually the minerals in the water turned her bones into stones. Being buried in the mud helped to fossilize her skeleton for it to come to Don's attention millions of years later.

Since he discovered Lucy, Don and other scientists have found other fossils of her species. In fact, in Ethiopia near where Lucy was found, Don and his team uncovered an entire group of individuals of all ages and sizes, adults and children, males and females, that they fondly called the "First Family." A scientist on Don's team found two fossil hominin teeth at the bottom of a hillside. Leg bones were seen higher up the hill. Because they were two right legs, Don realized that more than one individual was waiting to be uncovered. Site 333, as the hillside was called, revealed over two hundred fossil pieces representing thirteen individuals. These hominins were all lying close together, and there was no evidence of damage by hyenas. Don thinks this group died together in a catastrophe like a flash flood.

We now know certain things about Lucy's species. Males were much bigger than females; walking upright on two feet began well before brain size grew much bigger than that of apes; and stone tool use came even later than that. We also know that even though they were not yet human because of their small brain size, Lucy and her kind were the beginning of the social group we identify as *the human family*.

It took many years for scientists to clean, sort, and describe all the bones they found. But, like Lucy, the First Family members were on the way to being human because they walked upright on two feet. Paleoanthropologists have decided that walking upright is the first marker for becoming human. Early hominins may not have looked like us, but they are considered our ancestors because the changes of human evolution were beginning to take place.

Lucy defined both Don's past and his future at the same time. She represented his ancient human ancestor and the foundation for the development of his career. Don admits that his professional life has been a combination of luck and risk. He was lucky to glimpse Lucy when he was in the right place at precisely the right time. Any earlier than that exact moment, and she may still have been buried in the dirt; any later, and the torrential seasonal rains of Ethiopia might have washed her away. Don thinks he was also lucky that Lucy was given a name and not just a number. Most fossils are only numbered or identified according to where they were found. Having a cute woman's name bestowed a personality upon the fossil with which regular people could identify as a long-lost relative.

Don has no doubt that taking risks is an important part of being human. He took a huge risk traveling to Ethiopia as a young scientist with a brand-new doctoral degree. But he believed in his own intelligence and he trusted his ability. Africa was already known as the place where humanity originated. That led him to look in the right place for hominin fossils. Later, he took an even bigger risk in declaring that Lucy was a new species and in naming her species *Australopithecus afarensis* (pronounced aw-stray-lo-PITH-a-kus af-a-REN-sis). This new species changed the structure of the human family tree. Many scientists resisted the change at first. If Don had been wrong about this new species, he would have lost the respect of his colleagues. But again, he believed he was right and after finding more of Lucy's species as

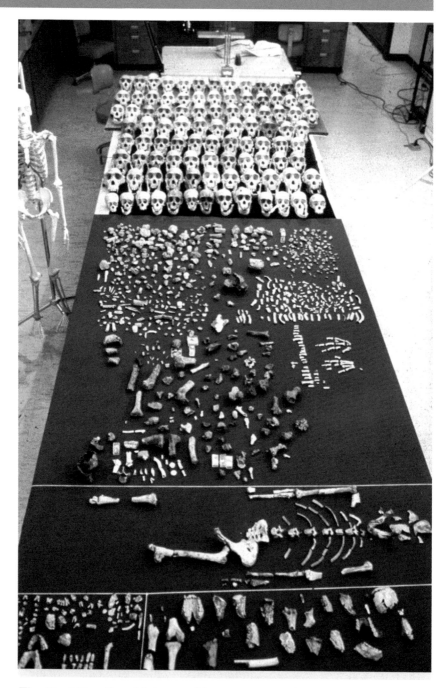

The First Family with Lucy sideways toward
the front and chimpanzee skulls in the back.
(Courtesy of Don Johanson/Institute of Human Origins)

confirmation, Don's addition to our family tree is now generally accepted in the science world today.

Let's see how discovering Lucy changed Don's life and how our lives have been changed because of what we now know about human evolution, thanks to both Lucy and Don.

NOTES

1. For a more detailed description of finding Lucy, in his own words, read Donald C. Johanson and Maitland Edey, *Lucy: The Beginning of Humankind* (New York: Simon & Schuster, 1981).

2. The First Family was featured in Donald C. Johanson, "Ethiopia Yields First 'Family' of Early Man," *National Geographic* 150, no. 6 (December 1976): 790–811.

3. Experience an interactive documentary about human evolution narrated by Don Johanson at http://www.becominghuman.org/.

Don, age about three, with his mother, Sally.
(Courtesy of Don Johanson)

CHILDHOOD IN CONNECTICUT

In 1925, a newly married couple left their native Sweden to immigrate to the United States. Sally and Carl Torsten Johanson settled in Chicago, Illinois, where Torsten worked as a barber. After eighteen years of marriage, Sally and Torsten joyously celebrated the birth of their first child, Donald Carl Johanson, on June 28, 1943. He was to be their only child, as Torsten died tragically after an accidental fall when Don was just two years old.

Sally's happy and comfortable life was turned upside down by her husband's death. She had to sell the family home and use up their bank savings to support herself and Don. Sally moved to Hartford, Connecticut, to be near relatives who had settled there. Lacking a formal education, Sally began working as a cleaning lady. She was not embarrassed about her position in life. Sally worked hard, never complained, and managed to maintain her household while raising her son.

SWEDISH IMMIGRATION

Young Swedes came to America in record numbers in the late 1800s and the early 1900s. It was a time of great human migration from Europe to North America. Sweden, in particular, was overcrowded and was running out of farmland. A serious famine killed many people. The wide-open spaces of the American Midwest looked like a good place for hungry, hardworking people to settle and establish farms. Most of these immigrants arrived in Chicago, which became one of the key hubs for immigrants to stop at as they found places to settle throughout the Midwest. For a while, Chicago was known for having the largest settlement of Swedish immigrants in the United States.

Besides farming, Swedish men found work in mining, lumbering, the railroad, and various skilled trades. Swedish women primarily were employed as domestic servants, such as cleaning ladies.

After World War II, Sweden became more modernized and the country's economy improved. Fewer young Swedes had to leave for a better life in America because they found many more opportunities in their own country. There are not many new Swedish immigrants anymore, but the second and third generations of those early immigrants are living throughout our country as American citizens.

In addition to Don Johanson, there have been numerous famous children or grandchildren of Swedish immigrants who have made significant contributions to our country and the world. These include:

Carl Sandburg (1878–1967), poet and author

Charles Lindbergh (1902–1974), pilot

William Rehnquist (1924–2005), chief justice of the US Supreme Court (1986–2005)

Edwin "Buzz" Aldrin (1930–), NASA *Apollo 11* astronaut

Candice Bergen (1946–), actress

CHILDHOOD

Don thrived on growing up in Hartford. He was always curious about the natural world and lived in a neighborhood with a nearby wooded area that was perfect for exploring. His group of friends mostly included children of other European immigrants who shared his interest in science. As a young boy, Don collected butterflies and enjoyed identifying animals, plants, and insects. Little did he know that he was actually studying biology.

Growing up as an only child, Don spent quite a bit of time by himself. Because he was intelligent and inquisitive, Don filled his time learning about science and his other major interest—music. The mother of one of his friends introduced him to classical music and opera. By the time he was a teenager, Don was saving whatever money he made from his paper route to go to the opera, a passion for which he maintains to this day.

LIFE IN THE 1940S

Life in America changed after World War II ended. As men went off to serve in the war, women filled their jobs and started working outside the home. Many women enjoyed their newfound economic independence. When the men returned from war, the government-sponsored GI Bill provided more of them than ever before with the opportunity and financial support to go to college.

Civil rights based on race and religion developed into a big issue as Americans became aware of the horrors of prejudice after the Holocaust. The United States was now a world super-power and worked with the countries destroyed by the war to rebuild their cities and their economies. In doing so, America's economy grew and prospered as Americans provided important materials to help Europe and Japan rebuild.

Childhood was different in postwar America, too. Don would leave his house in the morning and would stay outside all day exploring and playing, returning home only to eat and sleep. Parents did not have the same anxieties as today about bad people or harmful neighborhood influences preying on children, and they did not need to keep in constant contact with their kids. This was also a time when many mothers were at home to care for their children and the neighbors looked out for each other to protect and monitor children as they played. There was more opportu-nity for children to exercise and generate imaginative activities by themselves. Don found plenty of time to work on his butterfly collection and read his favorite books about science.

Don attended elementary school, junior high school, and high school in Hartford. Even though he was learning a great deal on his own, Don did not earn good grades at first. He enjoyed reading and learning, but he did not make the connection between his grades and his future. He performed poorly on stan-dardized tests, and a school counselor did not consider him "college material." By the middle of high school, Don finally realized on his own that the grades he earned mattered for what he would become after graduation. He was determined to work hard and go to college. He succeeded in achieving high marks and graduated with several awards.

Besides being interested in the science of biology, Don liked studying astronomy in school. He belonged to the astronomy club and enjoyed looking at the stars through the old telescope in his high school. Don was quite upset to find out that the old telescope would be left behind when the high school moved to a new building. He felt strongly that the telescope was an important part of his education. He appealed to the Hartford Board of Education and began a letter-writing campaign to local colleges and newspapers. Soon the board of education was receiving letters supporting the move of the telescope to the new high school.

Even though he was called into the principal's office and told that students should not interfere with adult business, Don did not give up. Eventually, the board of education relented and the telescope was moved. Don had taken the first of many big risks in his life, but he believed that he was right and that his effort was worth the result.

ROLE MODELS

Don had three people who were great influences in his early life. When he was around eight years old, Don met a man who was walking his dog in their neighborhood. He was Dr. Paul Leser, a scientist who specialized in anthropology, the study of the cultures and relationships of humankind. Leser befriended the fatherless boy and became his mentor. He shared his large library of science books with Don and fired up Don's imagination with fabulous tales of his adventures in Africa. Many years later, Don was able to return the favor by sharing his own amazing discoveries in Ethiopia. Leser was quite proud of his young friend as Don spread out the historic hominin fossils before him. Don dedicated his most recent book *Lucy's Legacy* to the memory of Paul Leser.

One of the science books Don read that became a major influence on his path in life was *Man's Place in Nature*, written by Thomas H. Huxley (1825–1895), another of his role models. Huxley was described as "Darwin's Bulldog" because he championed and defended Charles Darwin's newly developed theory of evolution during its early years, after Darwin published his major work *On the Origin of Species by Means of Natural Selection* (1859). This was at a time when many people criticized Darwin's views as being against the teaching of the Bible and rejected the view that humans, like all other species, developed over time and evolved to adapt to survive in their environment. Huxley gained fame in the late 1800s for cleverly speaking out on behalf of the more reserved Darwin. Huxley's book was the first to apply the theory of evolution to humans as members of the animal family and to stress that humans are part of nature.

Don's third early role model and influence was his mother. Sally showed Don that a person could accomplish a great deal if he or she worked hard enough. In the face of tragedy, losing her husband at a young age, Sally had the inner strength to confront the challenges of life. Her son paid attention, observed his mother's determination and ability to make her way in the world, and developed his own strong work ethic and ambitious plans for the future.

Sally never remarried or had any other children. She was dedicated to raising Don and supported his goals even as they changed throughout his life. She lived long enough to see her son become a successful scientist and was especially proud when he appeared on the news with veteran newscaster Walter Cronkite.

Walter Cronkite (1916–2009) was a noted news anchor for CBS and was widely regarded as "the most trusted man in America." He famously closed his news broadcast with the line "And that's the way it is…." The only time Cronkite changed his sign-off was when he reported about Lucy's discovery. That night Cronkite finished the newscast with, "And that's the way it

Paul Leser admiring the hominin fossils Don is showing him.
(Courtesy of Don Johanson)

Thomas H. Huxley, 1880.

Sally Johanson
as a young woman.
*(Courtesy of
Don Johanson)*

was...." Later, Walter Cronkite interviewed Don and paleoan-thropologist Richard Leakey, focusing on their different beliefs about the progress of human evolution. That eventful meeting is detailed in chapter 5.

Well before Don was appearing on television, when he was still sixteen, he knew he wanted to combine his interests in biology and anthropology. It was the late 1950s, and Don was reading about the first human fossils being found in Africa by the famous anthropologists Mary and Louis Leakey, Richard Leakey's parents. That is when Don decided to be a paleoanthro-

Don and Richard Leakey appearing with Walter Cronkite.
(Courtesy of the Institute of Human Origins)

pologist and study human evolution. Both Paul Leser and Sally encouraged him to go to college to study a more useful science, such as chemistry. Even though Don really wanted to study anthropology, he had done well in high school chemistry and was president of the chemistry club, so Don left for college intending to major in chemistry instead.

High school graduation portrait.
(Courtesy of Don Johanson)

CHEMIST OR PALEOANTHROPOLOGIST?

Although he was told as a schoolchild that he was not considered to be college material, after high school Don succeeded in being accepted by several colleges in the Midwest. He chose to go to the University of Illinois because it had a respected chemistry department and his godparents still lived in Chicago, the city of his birth. For two years, Don majored in chemistry while he took anthropology courses as electives and continued to read all he could about the subject on the side.

One day, while sitting in yet another chemistry class, Don realized that he wanted to be doing a more challenging, less defined type of science. He and his classmates were figuring out the solutions to problems, as classrooms full of students had done before them, using well-known formulas that appeared in the type of textbook with the answers already printed in the back of the book. Don craved a science that did not already have all the answers, because all the questions had not even been asked yet. He wanted to be the one figuring out the questions. Don took a

35

risk and changed his major to anthropology to explore human evolution.

As an undergraduate, Don went on several North American archeological digs. He primarily worked on excavating the remains of ancient Indian villages in Illinois but spent his twenty-first birthday digging in northern Arizona. He was excited to uncover evidence that humans had a great prehistory going back so many years. Don had made up his mind as a teenager that he wanted to find even older fossils than were available here, and he had his eyes set on Africa. When he took a short course from Dr. Louis Leakey, visiting at the university as a guest speaker, Don knew there was no turning back on his goal. Don graduated from the University of Illinois with a bachelor of arts in 1966 and proceeded to begin study in graduate school there.

Frustrated that the University of Illinois did not offer a program in human origins and that none of his professors went on digs to Africa, Don approached Dr. F. Clark Howell, a well-known professor at the University of Chicago who conducted fieldwork in Ethiopia. Dr. Howell was considered by many to be the father of modern paleoanthropology—the man who really helped create the field and expand it into a major academic discipline. Don took a risk and requested a meeting with Dr. Howell to tell him how interested he was in going to Africa to find human ancestor fossils. Dr. Howell apparently saw something in the daring and enthusiastic young man because he invited Don to study with him at the University of Chicago. Don transferred his graduate studies across to the other side of the city of his birth.

After a couple of years of hard work, Don was rewarded by an invitation from Dr. Howell to visit dig sites in Ethiopia. In 1970, at the age of twenty-seven, Don's childhood dream of

going to Africa finally came true. Not only did he have the opportunity to see the places where paleoanthropologists look for fossils, but he also visited Louis and Mary Leakey in Kenya, as well
as their son Richard, at that time a rising star in paleoanthropology. They generously shared their hominin fossil finds with
the inquisitive and eager student.

Don had to conduct quite a bit of research to become a
paleoanthropologist. To earn his master's degree in 1970, Don
prepared a thesis on chimpanzee molars. He expanded on this
research to write the dissertation for his doctorate on the entire
development of chimpanzee dentition (teeth). This proved to be
good preparation for examining the teeth of our human ancestors. Teeth are often the best-preserved part of a fossil, and

With Dr. Maurice Taieb in Hadar.
(Courtesy of the Institute of Human Origins)

The young scientist with the hominin knee joint he found in 1973.
(Courtesy of the Cleveland Museum of Natural History)

sometimes the only body part that remains of a particular individual. Teeth are covered by enamel, which is harder than bone and withstands fossilization well.

Before finishing his doctorate, though, Don returned to Ethiopia two more times. In 1972, Don took a chance and spent his only savings to join Maurice Taieb, a French geologist, in a groundbreaking survey of an unexplored region of Ethiopia. Dr. Taieb had visited an area of Ethiopia known as the Afar Triangle, which was located in the northern reaches of Africa's Great Rift Valley. The locality called Hadar caught Don's attention because its deep gorges exposed geological layers of sediment loaded with well-preserved fossils that were estimated to be more than three million years old. Although initially hopeful that they would find hominin fossils, Don returned from the expedition feeling disillusioned. It had been hot and demanding, the team had found plenty of animal fossils, but no hominin bones. To top it all off, Don had contracted malaria.

After recovering from both his malaria and his disappointment, Don returned to Hadar with Dr. Taieb in 1973. This time, he chanced upon a hominin knee joint. Don could tell by the way the lower end of the thighbone (femur) fit together with the upper end of the shinbone (tibia) that the creature these bones belonged to had walked upright on two feet. He did not find other parts of the skeleton to tell anything more about this individual, but it confirmed for Don that they were looking in the right place, and this find encouraged him to return the next year.

Don finished his doctoral dissertation during the summer of 1974. He left for Ethiopia in September, and by November had made his amazing discovery of Lucy. Don's early success in finding a hominin fossil changed the course of anthropological theory, and it also changed the direction his life would take in his career as a paleoanthropologist.

BECOMING A PALEOANTHROPOLOGIST

A paleoanthropologist is a special scientist who learns about human evolution by searching for and then studying the ancient, fossilized bones of our human ancestors. Don feels quite lucky to have found a hominin skeleton because many distinguished paleoanthropologists are not fortunate to discover any hominin fossils during their careers. Instead, they spend their professional lives researching and analyzing the information obtained by those who have discovered fossil remains.

Part explorers, part adventurers, paleoanthropologists face the unknown and have to ponder what happened to the fossils they find, what creatures they are holding, how they lived and died, and where they fit in our family tree. Ideas must be based on hard science in order to report honest and reliable research findings. Paleoanthropologists have to remain flexible and open-minded as new findings are revealed with the potential to transform the science. Lucy was just such a find.

After finding Lucy, Don returned to his job as curator of physical anthropology at the Cleveland Museum of Natural History and assistant professor at Case Western Reserve University in northeastern Ohio. Ethiopia allowed Don to bring Lucy's bones to the United States with the promise to eventually return her to the country of her origin. Don cleaned and studied Lucy's bones. He made casts of the fossil bones to share with other scientists so they could also learn from her.

Professor Johanson teaching anthropology
at Case Western Reserve University.
(Courtesy of Case Western Reserve University Archives)

A cast of a fossil is made by pressing it into clay. The clay impression is filled with plaster, silicone, or resin, which takes the shape of the fossil. Scientists try to make casts that keep all the important details of the original fossil. Ancient bones are often fragile. Making casts is a good way for many researchers to handle and study replicas of the real fossils.

As Dr. Clark Howell had been a mentor to Don, so too was Don a mentor to future paleoanthropologists—in particular, Dr. William (Bill) Kimbel, an accomplished scientist who took a course in anthropology from Professor Johanson while an undergraduate at Case. Bill is now one of Don's closest and most respected professional colleagues. Similar to Don, Bill went to college with a different career intention. He initially majored in psychology but became inspired by anthropology.

Bill believes it is important for a paleoanthropologist to be familiar with other sciences if he is to work effectively in the field today. That view is consistent with a tradition passed down by Don's mentor. Dr. Howell is credited with establishing a multidisciplinary approach to the field of paleoanthropology. In addition, Dr. Howell encouraged his fellow anthropologists to collaborate with a diverse group of scientists, including biologists, microbiologists, anatomists, botanists, geologists, and geneticists. Each science contributes a special expertise. Paleoanthropologists and anatomists know the bones, but geologists know about the age of rocks and volcanic history. Botanists have information about plant life in ancient times, while microbiologists and geneticists understand the secrets of our DNA. It often takes these specialists and others to interpret the numerous findings that are revealed by paleoanthropology.

Because so many types of science are involved in paleoanthropology, both Don and Bill encourage students to pursue a well-rounded undergraduate education, even majoring in biology, anatomy, or an earth science like geology, instead of anthropology. There is plenty of time to specialize in paleoanthropology in graduate school.

To truly understand finding fossils and the forces that act on them, students of paleoanthropology must travel to some of the roughest places on earth and spend a few months getting their hands dirty doing field exploration. So let's go on a dig.

Don and Dr. Bill Kimbel working in the field in Ethiopia, 1993.
(Courtesy of Nanci Kahn/Institute of Human Origins)

Positioning Lucy on a table after finding her in 1974.
(Courtesy of the Institute of Human Origins)

CHAPTER Four

SCIENTIST AND EXPLORER

D on never went camping as a child. In college he went on digs and camped in Illinois and Arizona, but he did not know what to expect from fieldwork in Africa. His fellow scientists figured that as a boy from the big city Don might not be tough enough for camping in the African desert. But Don quickly discovered that he loved everything about fieldwork and that it was his favorite part of being a paleoanthropologist.

Don enjoyed waking up in his tent while the desert air was still cool and the sun was just beginning to glow through the canvas above him. Don would lie on his cot listening as the camp would awaken to the smell of breakfast cooking and the quiet conversations of campmates around him. Not being much of a morning person, Don preferred the cool evenings as the sun was setting. He would walk out to a ridge, sit quietly by himself and just think while the surrounding mountains faded to purple.

Daytime in the African desert is harsh, dusty, and dry, with temperatures easily rising to 120 degrees Fahrenheit. Scorpions,

Bill Kimbel holding a newly discovered fossil.
(Courtesy of Don Johanson/Institute of Human Origins)

snakes, wild animals, and malarial mosquitoes are abundant and require constant attention. But daytime is when scientists look for fossils, and the middle of the desert is where the fossils wait to be found.

WHAT IS A FOSSIL?

A fossil is what is left of a living thing many years after it has died and hardened into rock. The fossil may be actual pieces of a plant or animal (usually the harder parts, such as the shell, skeleton, or teeth) or just the impression it leaves behind in the rock. To become fossilized, a dead organism must be buried quickly in sand, dirt, or other material before it decomposes or is eaten by another animal. Gradually, over millions of years, the fossil turns to rock as minerals replace the organic materials of the once-living thing. Over many more years, the hardened dirt may be eroded away to expose the fossils or bring them closer to the surface, where they may be discovered by scientists.

Some specialized geologists who focus on the composition and creation of rock formations are expert at locating the best places to search for fossils. They use aerial photography and satellite images to make maps of promising sites of eroding ground, where the underlying rock is exposed. Geologists also inform paleoanthropologists about the age of the rocks in which the fossils are found to help determine how old the fossils are. This is called stratigraphic dating. In most situations, the farther down the rock layers in which a fossil is found, the older that fossil is. These rock formations occur as a result of the layering of sediment and the decayed remains of plants and animals over many millions of years. Knowing the age of a fossil tells scientists a great deal about when an animal lived, in what kind of environment it lived, and how that fossil relates to other fossils found in the area.

During a dig, scientists come across the fossil remains of many different animals, including elephants, rhinoceroses, gazelles, and monkeys. Figuring out the age and types of animal fossils found in the dig area is called faunal dating or biostratigraphic analysis. For example, fossils of ancient hippopotami and crocodiles would signify that the area once was covered by an old swamp or lake, since this is the habitat of such creatures. The fossilized remains of primitive horses or giraffes would indicate the desert's previous life as an area of grassland in which these animals grazed.

In particular, the fossils of pigs that were known to have lived over three million years ago became pivotal in determining Lucy's age. The evolution of pigs over millions of years is well documented. Pigs were wide-ranging in Africa and left abundant fossils. Teeth, especially, from the ancient relatives of today's warthogs provide a reliable method for dating other fossils found near them.

Additional methods for establishing the age of a fossil include radiometric dating, such as potassium-argon dating. These measurements are done in a laboratory and are based on the natural transformation of certain elements found in either the fossils themselves or nearby rocks (such as the hardened lava from long-extinct volcanoes). Volcanic rocks contain radioactive potassium. As potassium decays, argon gas is released. The amount of these special elements changes over long periods of time at a regular rate that permits geologists to measure the age of rocks with precision. Carbon dating needs organic material and only extends back to between forty thousand and fifty thousand years. Another dating technique, paleomagnetism, uses the magnetic properties of the Earth to figure out the age of a fossil. Right now, the North Pole is positive while the South Pole is negative. Over millions of years, Earth has often reversed the poles of its internal magnet. By studying the way crystals have formed in rock, scientists know when the polarity of the Earth was normal (the magnetic reference was North) or reversed. Researchers can combine this information from the rock layer holding a fossil with all the other available methods and arrive at a reasonably accurate age estimate. At least one dating method must be used, but it is better for science results if several methods reach the same conclusion.

> **Much as they look and feel like rocks, fossils throb with a life of their own. They remind us of emotions and feelings almost inconceivably distant now, of satisfactions, fears, anger, and pain—all experienced by our own forebears. . . . What did the world really taste like on the tip of an old hominid tongue?**
>
> —DONALD C. JOHANSON, *Lucy*

When searching for fossils, Don stays aware that the bones and teeth he is handling were once from living creatures with working eyes and ears, with skin and muscles, and with blood pulsing through their bodies. Hominins may not have had the ability to think exactly as we do, but they experienced the world around them. To paleoanthropologists, hominin fossils are clues left behind by our ancestors that we can use to learn about their lives and about our origins.

After identifying a fossil location, scientists must secure per-

The dig starts with walking around looking for fossils.
A team member shows Don a fossil she found at the First Family site.
(Used by permission of David Brill)

mission to begin a dig from the country in which the fieldwork will be done. We must always remember that these researchers are guests in the countries where they conduct their on-site work. Most digs last for a few months, depending on the weather and how much funding the scientists were able to obtain to pay the expenses of an expedition. In Africa, the best time to do fieldwork is during one of the dry seasons, late winter, early spring, or fall. Digs are frequently scheduled for the most reliable dry season in the fall. Because there are few roads in the desert and the terrain

When a fossil is found, the area is marked off with a grid.
(Courtesy of Don Johanson/Institute of Human Origins)

is rough, scientists get around in the dry streambeds with four-wheel drive vehicles like Land Rovers. During the heavy rainy season, the beds would be full of rushing water, and it would be difficult to access the fossils.

DIGGING IN THE DESERT

A dig starts with a walking survey of the area. It takes a person with sharp eyes to spot the bones lying among the rocks, and with

Don in 1974 carefully excavating the dirt from one of Lucy's bones.
(Courtesy of the Institute of Human Origins)

a light step, so as not to crush the fragile fossils. Looking for bones in the desert is a lot like being on the watch for an interesting shell at the beach. You have to walk bent over at the waist with your eyes scanning left and right while placing your feet carefully.

A GPS device (a global positioning system, the same as the one in our cars) is employed to designate the spot where a hominin fossil is found. The spot is photographed and identified with a locality number while the area is marked off with nails and twine to form a square grid on the ground. Then the slow, steady work of excavation begins.

A surface search is conducted over the ground while on your

The excavated dirt is gathered in buckets.
(Courtesy of Don Johanson/Institute of Human Origins)

The dirt is sifted through window mesh screens
to find even the smallest teeth and pieces of bone.
(Courtesy of Don Johanson/Institute of Human Origins)

Carefully cleaning the fossil skull of a First Family child.
(Used by permission of David Brill)

hands and knees, crawling one foot at a time. Any bone fragment found is picked up and sorted into either hominin or other animal. After the surface is clear, whisk brooms are used to gently sweep up one thin layer of dirt at a time from each square in the grid. The dirt is placed in shallow metal pans to be examined for fossils. The collected dirt is sifted through a handmade sieve. A two-foot-square wooden tray with a window mesh screen for a bottom has handles attached so two people can shake the tray back and forth. After the dirt drops through, even the smallest piece of bone or tooth will remain on the screen. Teeth are the body part most frequently found because, as was mentioned earlier, tooth enamel is harder than bone and therefore lasts longer. Small rock hammers are wielded to loosen up more compact dirt as the dig progresses lower into the ground. The process of hunting for fossils requires patience and a good eye to sort the gathered material one piece at a time. It can take weeks of this work until the paleoanthropologists are satisfied that they have found all of the fossil bits available in that spot.

The bones and teeth are taken back to camp, where they are cleaned and laid out to identify them and put them together in some order. Sometimes a dig will yield hundreds of pieces. Don's colleague Bill Kimbel likens putting fossil bones together to completing a giant jigsaw puzzle. Unfortunately, this puzzle often has many pieces missing or the edges of the puzzle pieces are broken or worn away. Bill's favorite part of being a paleoanthropologist is reconstructing once-living creatures from the newly discovered bones they left behind. Although a tedious and time-consuming part of the job, the attention to detail in assembling bone pieces can be quite rewarding. Bill once built a skull of Lucy's species, *Australopithecus afarensis*, with the help of another

Bill Kimbel reconstructing the skull of *Australopithecus afarensis.*
(Courtesy of Enrico Ferorelli)

scientist, from over one hundred pieces of broken skulls from several males.

Don describes the actual dig as "back-breaking, knee-scuffing manual labor" of which he loves every minute, especially when the entire field team cheers each time a piece of hominin bone is found. When the field camp breaks up, Don feels a bit sad and wistfully says good-bye to the people and the land.

THE FIELD CAMP

A field expedition is more than just collecting fossils and mapping sites, it also involves repairing vehicles and keeping everyone in camp fed and safe. Although the basic tools of excavation have not changed much during Don's career, some of the camp amenities have. For a while, the heavy green canvas tents were replaced by light nylon dome tents. Green canvas tents are back in style again because it was determined that they last longer than the nylon ones. A major technological improvement includes the use of solar panels to provide power for computers and lamps.

Extinct hominins used to live around the edges of an ancient lake that once covered the desert where Don found Lucy. The lake shrank and dried up as the climate changed over millions of years, leaving just the Awash River wending through the beige and gray valley of Hadar. Modern-day hominins now set up their campsites along the edge of the river. The water in the river is fine for bathing, but it has to be filtered for drinking and cooking. Don is always extra cautious when going for a swim because the descendants of the crocodile Lucy may have encountered might still live in the river.

Field camp on the edge of the Awash River.
(Used by permission of David Brill)

Besides several private personal tents, the field camp features one or two large, open tents with side flaps. One tent provides a shady place for eating meals and meeting, while another one can be used for a field laboratory. A camp cook prepares meals out in the open, usually with the main ingredient of goat because that is what is most available. But there is always fresh baked bread, peanut butter, and plenty of Kool-Aid to replenish fluids lost while sweating in the hot sun. At the edge of camp is a grass-lined hut affectionately known as the Lucy Club. Inside, a small field laboratory is set up for scientists to begin studying the hominin bones and teeth found so far on the expedition.

An important part of going on a dig in a foreign country is getting to know the local inhabitants. Don has made a point of befriending the Afar tribesmen in the desert. The Afar are nomadic Muslims (adherents of the Islamic faith) who are usually not friendly to outsiders. They carry rifles to defend themselves from rival tribes as they herd their livestock, usually goats, around the desert. While the scientists are in camp, the Afar act as guards using their rifles to protect the camp, and they are happy to sell their goats to the camp cook. In addition, some members of the tribe do work around the camp or help look for fossils.

When the field season is complete, the bones are taken back to the scientists' laboratory, depending upon the agreement with the country in which they were found. Ethiopia now has its own laboratory for studying fossils found in that country. The original Lucy is housed at the National Museum of Ethiopia in the capital, Addis Ababa. In the lab, fossils are analyzed to more accurately determine how old they are. They are measured and plaster casts are made to share with other scientists for study. Researchers frequently consult the sketches they drew in the

An Afar tribesman with his herd of goats.
(Courtesy of Don Johanson/Institute of Human Origins)

field, the photographs taken, and the journals in which they recorded their notes. The new fossils are compared with other fossils to identify them with a known species, or, as with Lucy, to realize the discovery of a new species. This process encompasses

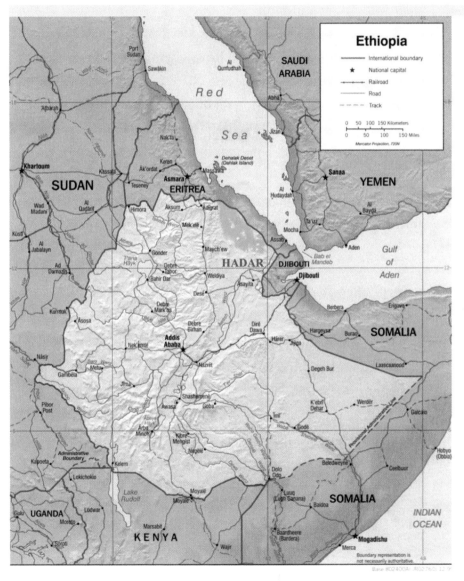

Ethiopia with Hadar in red.
(CIA, University of Texas Libraries, 1999)

several years of work. All the findings are written up in articles submitted to scientific journals to share the information with the broader scientific community. Paleoanthropologists disclose their new fossil findings at scientific meetings, press conferences, student lectures, and presentations to the general public.

Each paleoanthropologist has special places where he or she prefers to conduct fieldwork. Other scientists respect these sites as established bases and look elsewhere for fossils in unexplored areas. Don and Bill have been on digs around the world in China, Tunisia, Israel, Iran, Kenya, and Tanzania. However, both of them say their favorite place to conduct fieldwork is Ethiopia. Not only do they enjoy the friendliness of the people there, but they appreciate the amazing number of hominin fossils they have found in what Bill calls an "invaluable scientific resource."

ETHIOPIA AND DINKINESH

Scientists now know that it is extremely likely that human beings, as we know them, began in Africa and spread into the Middle East, Europe, and Asia. It is appropriate that Don found Lucy waiting for him in Ethiopia. Don thinks that Lucy has become much more famous than he is around the world, but especially in Ethiopia, where she is considered a national treasure. The Ethiopians have given her the name Dinkinesh, which means "she is wonderful" in the native language of Amharic (pronounced am-HAR-ick). The Afar call her Heelomali (pronounced hee-low-MA-lee) for "she is special."

Ethiopia is a landlocked country located in the Horn of Africa. It is situated where three tectonic plates (layers) of Earth's crust meet. This juncture of the African, Arabian, and Indian plates forms the Great Rift Valley. The area has active earthquakes and volcanoes. Ethiopia is characterized by tree-covered mountains and barren deserts. With a landmass that is about two times the size of Texas, Ethiopia is home to eighty-five million people.

The Ethiopian people are culturally diverse, with over one hundred different ethnic groups and tribes, seventy different languages, and four different religions. One-half of all Ethiopians are Christian. They believe that the Ark of the Covenant, holding two stones inscribed by God with the Ten Commandments, was brought from Jerusalem to Ethiopia in olden times. This Christian artifact is kept securely guarded in a church located in the city of Axum.

Unfortunately, the Christian nation has endured an unending quarrel with its Muslim neighbors. The country has a long history of war and political turmoil. For centuries, Ethiopia was ruled by a series of kings and emperors. In the late 1800s, this region was discovered by European explorers, and various countries—including Portugal, Great Britain, and Italy—tried unsuccessfully to colonize it. The Ethiopians fought European control and finally secured true independence in the early 1940s.

In 1930, the reign of the last emperor, Haile Selassie (pronounced HIGH-lee sell-AH-see), began. While exerting total control, Selassie has been credited with modernizing the country, adding hospitals and schools, and trying to improve the economy. Regrettably, he was not concerned with the well-being of all the people, and hundreds of thousands of Ethiopians died in a dreadful famine. In 1974, Selassie was removed from power by a socialist military government called the Derg. Ethiopia sided more with the Soviet Union than with the United States during this Cold War era. After World War II, the United States and the Soviet Union did not actively fight with each other. Instead, the two superpowers did not agree on economic and political policies and lived in a state of tension until the Soviet Union collapsed into separate countries in 1991.

Meanwhile, the Ethiopian people were plagued by worsening violence from their own government, from rival tribes fighting for power, and from wars that developed with their neighbors to the north and east in the Horn of Africa, Eritrea and Somalia. Another countrywide famine caused more deaths from hunger and disease. The country became closed to outsiders, including scientists. Because Don was unable to conduct fieldwork at Hadar during this period, he had the opportunity to go on digs in other countries. He also took the time to study thoroughly all his fossil finds and to write his bestselling book, *Lucy: The Beginnings of Humankind.* Sadly, Don ended up having to stay away from Hadar longer than he would have liked.

In the 1990s, a democratic government was elected by the people of Ethiopia with a constitution that gave rights to the wide variety of ethnic groups. With less internal strife, the country once again opened to foreign tourists and international scientists. After enduring an eight-year ban on fossil expeditions, Don was able to return to Hadar in 1990.

Ethiopia still is one of the poorest countries in the world. Its people have a low life expectancy and many suffer from malnutrition, poor sanitation, infectious diseases (including AIDS), and inadequate healthcare. The Ethiopian economy is based on agriculture, especially coffee, of which it is the largest producer in Africa. Over time, the Ethiopians have removed so many trees in their attempt to increase the amount of available farmland that their environment is now suffering greatly. Loss of the forest causes a decline in wildlife, while the exposed soil erodes away into the expanding desert. Hunger is prevalent because of over-population and drought. As an established democracy, Ethiopia is now considered a friend of the United States, and we are one of the main countries providing food aid for its people.

The young democracy is trying to improve educational opportunities for its people. One of its goals is for all children to go to school, especially girls, who have not traditionally been allowed an education. Ethiopia needs to work harder to improve its human rights record because its military somewhat limits the freedom of the press and suppresses freedom of speech, but it has become an important ally against the threat of Islamic terrorists.

The Ethiopians are proud of their heritage and are interested in sharing it with the world. Notably, Ethiopia is the site of some of the oldest hominin fossils and the oldest stone tools known at present. In Hadar, the original lakes and forests are long gone, leaving behind in the mud, silt, and volcanic ash remnants of the creatures and humans who lived, died, and evolved there many millennia ago.

NOTES

1. Don tells the exciting and rewarding story of the 1986 field season where he went when he was unable to conduct field research in Ethiopia in Donald C. Johanson and James Shreeve, *Lucy's Child: The Discovery of a Human Ancestor* (New York: William Morrow, 1989).

2. The culture and the people of Ethiopia are fully described in Steven Gish, Winnie Thay, and Zawiah Abdul Latif, *Ethiopia* (New York: Marshall Cavendish Benchmark, 2007).

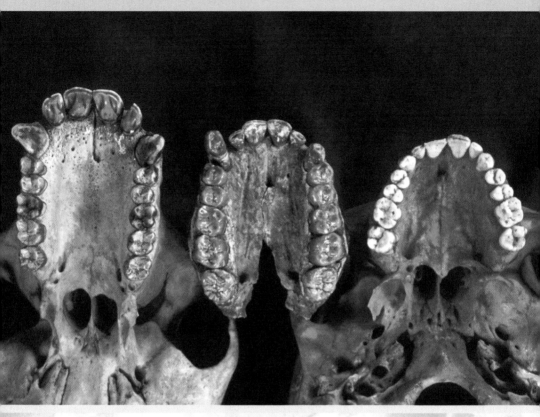

Comparison of upper jaws of chimpanzee,
Australopithecus afarensis, and *Homo sapiens* to demonstrate how
Lucy's dentition was in transition between ape and human.
(Courtesy of William H. Kimbel/Institute of Human Origins)

CHAPTER Five

THE EVOLUTION OF MONARCHS AND MANKIND

We cannot fully grasp who we are as a species until we have a more complete knowledge of our evolutionary roots.

—Donald C. Johanson

As a young boy, Don was fascinated that the evolutionary process responsible for the monarch butterfly in his collection and the rabbits in his neighborhood is the same natural force that gave rise to human beings. Evolution is responsible for the wonderful diversity of all life on Earth. In fact, humans share some genetic material with every form of life that ever has existed or continues to exist.

Evolution is how new species develop through genetic change. Scientists do not all agree about whether that process takes place gradually and in small steps or occurs in short bursts with long periods of no change in the intervals. But all scientists agree that all life-forms have changed over vast periods of time. No one in the field disputes that evolution takes place. To date,

Charles Darwin, 1880.

no other scientific theory besides Darwin's evolution by natural selection has been able to explain satisfactorily how life on Earth became so complex and varied.

Charles Darwin (1809–1882) was an English naturalist who dared to publish his theory of natural selection, which states that living things with the ability to adapt to a changing environment will be naturally selected to survive and reproduce. Parents pass on certain adaptations (modifications) through their genes to their offspring that allow their children to survive and reproduce, while the parents of other species are less able to adapt to their environments and so eventually die off and become extinct. After many generations of successful adaptations, a new species different from the original one evolves.

Genes are the basic units of inheritance in the cells of our bodies that we receive from our parents. Genes are composed of paired and spiraled strands of DNA (deoxyribonucleic acid) that instruct our cells on how to function. When a new living thing is being formed, the DNA makes copies of itself to pass along. Sometimes mutations, or random changes, occur in the copying process and the resulting cell will be slightly different. If the mutation results in offspring that are better suited to their surroundings or more attractive to mates, those traits will continue to be selected and show up in subsequent generations.

Because we look so similar to the African apes, Darwin proposed the idea in 1871 that humans and apes shared a common ancestor in the distant past. Scientists now know that living things that resemble each other tend to have more genes in common. Humans share more genes with chimpanzees than with any other animal. Darwin also suggested that all humans evolved in Africa, which we now know almost certainly to be true as well.

Langdon Smith (1858–1908), an American poet and contemporary of Darwin wrote a poem called "Evolution," an excerpt of which underscores how strong an impact Darwin's theory had on the times:

> When you were a tadpole and I was a fish
> In the Paleozoic time,
> And side by side on the ebbing tide
> We sprawled through the ooze and slime,
> Or skittered with many a caudal flip
> Through the depths of the Cambrian fen,
> My heart was rife with the joy of life,
> For I loved you even then.

Don sitting in Darwin's study at Down House, England, 1988.
(Courtesy of Lenora Carey)

Don understands that the issue of drawing a line between apes and humans is scientifically complicated and emotionally difficult for most people. The acceptance of human evolution requires understanding that humans evolved from lower life-forms in an unplanned and not divine way. It also is an enormous challenge for paleoanthropologists to figure out when the transition from ape to hominin took place. Don is convinced, however, that no one should feel awkward about our evolutionary past. Instead, we should call upon it to better realize that we are interconnected with all of nature. If we can acknowledge that we are intricately related to all other life on our planet, perhaps we will care more about our fellow creatures, with which we share so many genes.

THE LANGUAGE OF PALEOANTHROPOLOGY

Just as reconstructing shattered pieces of fossil is like assembling a jigsaw puzzle, so too are Lucy and her species proving to be integral pieces of a puzzle in understanding our picture of the human family tree. Scientists share information and debate their positions from a common language that includes the naming of species. As we have seen, Lucy's species is called *Australopithecus afarensis* and holds a central branch on the human family tree. How did she get that name?

Naming a Species

A Swedish scientist named Carl Linnaeus developed a system in 1735 for classifying and naming all the plants and animals of the world. In his system, each organism receives a two-part name. The first name refers to genus, a more general group with many characteristics in common, while the second name indicates the species, a more specific reference to individuals who are related or are capable of breeding with each other. Names are selected from Greek or Latin sources. Linnaeus himself put humans as part of the animal kingdom and gave us our binomial name *Homo sapiens* ("wise man"). Don used the Linnaean system when naming Lucy's species. *Australopithecus* means "southern ape." *Afarensis* means "from Afar."

How a Species Is Categorized

	Humans	**Lucy**
Kingdom:	Animalia	Same
Phylum:	Chordata (spinal cord)	Same
Class:	Mammalia	Same
Order:	Primates	Same
Family:	Hominidae	Same
Tribe:	Homininae	
	(upright walking)	Same
Genus:	*Homo*	*Australopithecus*
Species:	*sapiens*	*afarensis*

Even if it be granted that the difference between man and his nearest allies is as great in corporeal structure as some naturalists maintain, and although we must grant that the difference between them is immense in mental power . . . as it appears to me, in the plainest

matter, that man is descended from some
lower form, notwithstanding that connecting
links have not hitherto been discovered.

—CHARLES DARWIN, *THE DESCENT OF MAN*, 1871

CONNECTING LINKS

In popular language, the quest for a *missing link* is often mentioned. That term implies that scientists are searching for one fossil of a half-ape, half-human creature to answer all questions about the origins of humans. The truth is much more complicated. Hominins are interrelated and connected in diverse ways. Many important fossils provide material for creating, analyzing, and discussing the place all known hominins hold in human evolution.

The progression of early hominin fossils shows a gradual change from apelike creatures to more humanlike creatures over millions of years. Some scientists believed that our ancestors first evolved a larger brain on their way to becoming human. Lucy and her species still had a small apelike brain, but they clearly were walking on humanlike legs and feet, confirming the idea that we stood up before we grew big brains.

As further confirmation of Don's findings, in 1978 a path of footprints was found in Tanzania by Mary Leakey's team. Over three million years ago, in a place now called Laetoli, two hominins walked through freshly fallen volcanic ash. Their footsteps, preserved when the ash hardened into rock, show upright walking with a humanlike gait, not with a bent knee, chimpanzee-like gait. It has since been determined that the footprints likely belong to *Australopithecus afarensis*. Therefore, Lucy's species had feet with a straight big toe and an arch, just like humans.

Scientists recognize three primary physical characteristics that separate hominins from apes—upright walking, larger brain capacity, and jaw structure (including teeth). Which of those characteristics came first, how they came about, and which was most important in making us human have been the subjects of immense debate over the years and still occupy much scholarly effort. Lucy and other famous fossils discovered since Darwin's day have answered many questions in this regard.

THE HUMAN FAMILY TREE

A human family tree helps to organize our knowledge of our origins into a simplified and logical order. But it must remain flexible and be redrawn if necessary as new evidence arises. Our understanding of the family tree is becoming more complex as more fossil species are revealed. Some scientists observe that it has become more of a "bush" of life because so many branches have been added. Some of these branches eventually led to humans, but all others ended in extinction.

Scientists continue to debate whether certain species deserve a spot on the tree. Initially, when Don found Lucy, other scientists believed she was a variety of *Australopithecus africanus* and not a new species. Lucy did not have a complete skull, and it was not until 1992 that an *Australopithecus afarensis* skull with obvious differences from *africanus* was found to prove they were separate species. As a result, *africanus* is now on a side branch, probably evolving into other hominins before that line went extinct. One thing is clear, though. Today's family trees all place Lucy's

HUMAN FAMILY TREE

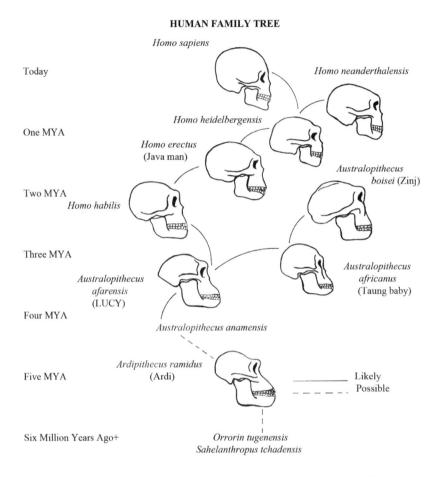

Human Family Tree. *(Illustration by CAP Saucier)*

species, *Australopithecus afarensis*, in a preeminent position on the branch leading to the development of humans.

Before Hominins

In the Miocene era (between twenty-three million and five million years ago), there were many types of apes living in the thick forests of the world. About five million years ago, the climate of

Africa became drier. The forests shrank and lakes began to disappear, while grasslands began to appear. Many ape species went extinct, but those that adapted to the changing environment survived and eventually evolved into modern-day apes and humans.

Today there are only five types of apes in the world—gibbons, orangutans, gorillas, chimpanzees (including bonobos), and humans. Based on the analysis of our human DNA, geneticists have determined that we last shared a common ancestor with gibbons twenty million years ago, with orangutans sixteen million years ago, with gorillas about ten million years ago, and with chimpanzees (our closest relative) six to seven million years ago. While we share 98 percent of our genes with chimpanzees, we did not evolve directly from them, nor will they necessarily evolve into humans. Rather, at one point in the past we had an ancestor in common that evolved in at least two different directions and probably was quite different from either humans or today's chimpanzees. Our last common ancestor probably looked more apelike, with a smaller brain and larger face and teeth than us. But this creature likely was beginning to develop a shorter and wider pelvis with hip and knee joints more like humans, which allowed it to walk on two feet.

All the fossils since the human branch split from the apes are considered hominins, characterized by being upright walkers that are beyond apes, although some were not quite human. The challenge for paleoanthropology is to figure out which of the known hominin species survived to evolve into humans. It is not practical to catalogue all known hominin fossil finds here, but our family tree represents one accepted scientific version and features the main characters including the early hominins, the australopithecines, and our *Homo* ancestors.

Earliest Hominins

Paleoanthropology is more than the manual labor of digging for fossils; it also requires a good deal of thinking and analyzing of the fossil evidence to reach well-thought-out hypotheses about what our ancestors might have been like. Scientists must speculate about the behavior of hominins based only on the bones themselves because behaviors do not fossilize. Don has wondered for a long time what caused our first ancestor to walk on two feet, since it is not the fastest way to move around. Animals run much faster on four feet. The first hominins began upright walking perhaps because it allowed them to use their arms in gathering more food and carrying it back to share with mates and children. These activities led to the formation of more human behaviors, such as pair bonding (mating), group cooperation, and nurturing of the young in families.

Upright walking is certainly older than Lucy and now can be traced back to six million years ago. Researchers have discovered a few hominin fossil pieces that may be up to seven million years old. None of these older fossils is as complete as Lucy, but some may represent her ancestors. Two species of hominin in particular are but fragments of bone, and it is less clear where they fit in the developing picture of human evolution. These intriguing hominins are *Orrorin tugenensis* ("dawn" or "original man" from the Tugen Hills in Kenya, six million years old; pronounced or-OR-in too-gen-EN-sis), and *Sahelanthropus tchadensis* ("human" from Sahel in Chad, in central Africa, six to seven million years old; pronounced saw-hel-AN-throw-pus chad-EN-sis). One or both of them may have begun upright walking.

A third early hominin of importance is *Ardipithecus ramidus* ("ground root ape," pronounced r-dee-PITH-a-kus RAM-eh-dus), at 4.4 million years old. A team led by Dr. Timothy White recently announced its findings in 2009 on "Ardi," a mostly complete, reconstructed skeleton of an upright-walking hominin that is older than Lucy. Found in Ethiopia in 1992 with over thirty other individuals of her species, Ardi's bones were crushed and fragile. It took scientists over fifteen years to restore her skeleton. Ardi is quite apelike, with long arms and feet that show a splayed-out big toe that can grasp tree branches.

Some scientists are skeptical that Ardi walked upright on those feet. Don believes that Ardi is an amazing fossil find, but he is not convinced that she is a direct ancestor to humans. Lucy's species goes back to 3.7 million years ago, and that is too short a time for the changes to take place for Ardi's species to evolve into Lucy's species. Scientists will debate for a long while whether Ardi is a human ancestor or a dead-end branch on the human family tree.

Australopithecines

Lucy's jaw and teeth can be described as partway between ape and human. Her teeth are smaller than an ape's, but her jaw is not as rounded as a human jaw. An ape's teeth are generally larger, especially the canines in males, and the rows of teeth on the side are parallel. Don's early education in chimpanzee teeth came in handy when studying and identifying the fossilized teeth he found. By the character of the teeth, jaw, and small brain capacity, Don knew he could not claim Lucy and her species as human, but they certainly were on the way there.

Don's discovery of *Australopithecus afarensis* not only transformed the shape of the human family tree but also caused great controversy in the paleoanthropological community. Many scientists, including the Leakeys, did not want to believe that humans evolved from such a primitive animal as Lucy. The Leakey group insisted that humans evolved at an earlier time from a species of *Homo* as yet unfound that existed before *Australopithecus* and was on a different evolutionary track than the australopithecines. They believed that australopithecines evolved separately from early humans.

Don had been close to the Leakey family. Early in his career, Don considered Richard Leakey a friendly rival. The two often disagreed about fossils, but Don enjoyed exchanging ideas with Richard. Their friendship began to deteriorate after Don named the new species. When Richard and Mary attacked Don's proof for Lucy's placement on the human family tree, the dispute turned somewhat bitter. Don valued his friendship with the Leakeys and was sad to lose it. Nonetheless, Don strongly defended his evidence that *Australopithecus afarensis* was indeed a human ancestor and not a side branch on the tree. The skeletons of Lucy and the First Family were so much like our own and showed the first signs of being humanlike. After studying them for years, Don was convinced that *afarensis* was on the direct line to humans.

In 1981, a final falling out between Don and Richard would take place over a dispute about the human family tree. Walter Cronkite invited Don and Richard to appear on his *Universe* television series. Prepared to discuss evolution, Don arrived with a chart of his version of the human family tree and an *afarensis* skull. Richard did not want to argue with Don about their different viewpoints, but Cronkite turned the show into a debate.

Don and Richard Leakey appearing at a joint news conference in Washington, DC, to talk about their discoveries, 1976.
(Used by permission of Bettman/CORBIS)

After defacing Don's chart and refusing to give his own interpretation of the human family tree, Richard left the show angrily. He and Don have barely exchanged words since then.

Fortunately for science, paleoanthropologists are still finding fossils of *Australopithecus afarensis*. In 2000, across the river from Hadar, a young Ethiopian scientist named Zeresenay Alemseged (pronounced zer-EZ-in-ay a-LEM-sa-ged) found the skeleton of a three-year-old female that is now called the Dikika baby (pronounced dah-KEE-kah). Even though the Dikika baby was born one hundred and twenty thousand years before Lucy, and Don does not know for sure whether Lucy ever had a baby, the media called the Dikika baby "Lucy's Child." A few babies among the members of the First Family were helpful in learning more about the Dikika baby.

Dr. Alemseged benefited from a recent trend to educate native Africans about their own prehistory. Don and other prominent scientists have made special efforts to bring Ethiopians into the field of paleoanthropology in their homeland.

There was evidence available before the discovery of Lucy that hominin evolution was initially characterized by upright walking as well as smaller teeth and a smaller jaw. In 1924, Dr. Raymond Dart discovered the first hominin fossil found in Africa. The more than two-million-year-old skull, named the Taung child, was found in a cave in South Africa. The Taung child had a small skull and inner brain case, but the position of the hole at the base of the skull where the spinal cord would have entered the brain (foramen magnum) suggested that the skull was balanced on top of an upright creature. The foramen magnum in apes and other animals that walk on four feet is located farther to the back of the head. Moreover, the tooth structure was not ape-like. The canine teeth were not fangs, and the other teeth were smaller than apes'.

Dart was criticized for claiming that the fossil was a hominin, and the Taung skull was ridiculed as being nothing more than a baby ape. Scientists have since determined that this fossil represented *Australopithecus africanus* (pronounced af-ri-CAWN-us), a species that probably evolved from *Australopithecus afarensis*. But unlike Lucy's species, the Taung child's line apparently did not lead to humans. More likely it evolved into two species—*Australopithecus boisei* (named after a benefactor, Charles Boise) and *Australopithecus robustus* ("large")—both of which eventually went extinct.

Fossils of hominins that lived after Lucy have reinforced that

Don holding the skull of the Taung baby in South Africa.
(*Courtesy of the Institute of Human Origins*)

Australopithecus afarensis is ancestral to humans. Other more recent finds have connected Lucy's species securely to our past. In 1994, Meave Leakey (Richard's wife) uncovered the remains of *Australopithecus anamensis* ("southern ape of the lake"; pronounced an-na-MEN-sis) dated at four million years old, more than a half million years before Lucy. Based on a shinbone, Meave determined that this species walked upright. Analysis of teeth and jaws that Meave collaborated on with Don confirmed that it was an ancestor to Lucy's species, *Australopithecus afarensis.*

Great controversy often erupts in paleoanthropology when a new species is announced. This was the case when, from two skeletons found in a cave in South Africa that are nearly two million years old, Dr. Lee Berger proclaimed a new species, *Australopithecus sediba* ("fountain"; pronounced sah-DEE-bah). The first fossil was actually found by Dr. Berger's nine-year-old son.

Two million years ago, australopithecines and early *Homo*, our genus, were living at the same time. Different body parts changed at different times in human evolution, for instance, legs advanced before arms, and the pelvis transformed before the brain. Defining the exact point when australopithecines transitioned into *Homo* is difficult. *Sediba* shares many advanced traits of *Homo*, such as small teeth and face shape, but still has some primitive characteristics of the smaller-brained, longer-armed australopithecines. Dr. Berger believes that *sediba* may have evolved from *Australopithecus africanus*. According to Don, that would place the new species on an evolutionary dead end.

Don and Bill Kimbel feel the new species would fit better in the *Homo* genus. Perhaps the excavation of more fossils of this species will determine its placement. Although other *Homo* species existing at the same time as *sediba* were more advanced,

Don thinks that any information about a new *Homo* species would help to establish the connection between *Australopithecus afarensis* and early *Homo*.

Homo

Lucy and the other australopithecines did not have a brain large enough to be considered human. But their descendants gradually developed a higher and rounder skull with a larger brain case, a more prominent chin, and a less pronounced eyebrow ridge. Our genus *Homo* (again, meaning "man") first appeared over two million years ago. Based on the appearance of australopithecine teeth, scientists know that the australopithecines were primarily vegetarians. It is likely that *Homo* had a diet consisting of more energy-rich protein from eating meat, which led to the evolution of the larger brain. A bigger brain permits more expedient hunting and scavenging.

In 1972, Richard Leakey found a skull in Kenya that was first classified as *Homo habilis* but is now known as *Homo rudolfensis* (from Lake Rudolf in Kenya). It eventually was found to be 1.8 million years old. Years later, in 1986, Don Johanson and Bill Kimbel worked on an excavation in Tanzania of the first specimen of *Homo habilis* that included fragments of a skull and bones from the body. Together they concluded that although *Homo habilis* had a larger brain and a more humanlike jaw and teeth than *Australopithecus afarensis*, the body was similar enough to prove that Lucy was, in fact, an ancestor of humans. *Homo habilis* is distinguished by evidence that members of this species had begun to make and use stone tools, thus the name meaning "handy man."

Often, evolution takes place slowly with small changes made

at a time, but once in a while, extreme climate variations can cause evolution to speed up. As the African climate dried and grasslands transformed into desert, the first humans were forced to adapt to the new environment. There are but two hundred thousand years between *Homo habilis* and *Homo erectus* ("upright man," also known as *Homo ergaster*, Greek for "workman"), but the evolution from *habilis* to *erectus* carried with it a big leap in brain and body size. *Homo erectus* was much more like modern humans and was the first hominin to travel outside Africa. Fossil bones of this species have been found in Europe, the Middle East, and China.

The most famous fossil of *Homo erectus* was found on the island of Java off of Southeast Asia in 1891. Many people at that time thought incorrectly that humans originated in Asia, so Eugene Dubois set out to find human ancestors there. Dubois luckily discovered the "Java man" skull and thighbone estimated to be one million years old. Before Dubois, scientists had not been actively seeking out our ancient ancestors. Perhaps his greatest contribution to paleoanthropology was inspiring so many scientists to follow him into the adventure of searching for fossils.

Paleoanthropology is an active science that must constantly update information as new fossils are discovered. Recent *Homo habilis* and *Homo erectus* fossils found by Meave Leakey in Kenya indicate that these two species may have overlapped in time and place. In other words, they may have existed at around the same time and lived in the same general region. It is exciting to consider that *erectus* might not have evolved from *habilis*, but that they actually shared a common ancestor from which they both evolved. That means that an as-yet-unknown early *Homo* species, probably descended from the australopithecines, is still out there and is waiting to be found.

Homo erectus continued to evolve outside of Africa, and this line survived for quite a long time. Scientists are nearly certain, however, that the *Homo erectus* hominins who remained in Africa, and which are now classified as *Homo ergaster*, are those who successfully progressed in the climb up the family tree to modern humans.

Homo antecessor ("pioneer man") dated from eight hundred thousand years ago followed *Homo erectus*. Then, five hundred thousand years ago, *Homo heidelbergensis* (from Heidelberg, Germany) came on the scene. These hominins left evidence of more sophisticated tools, such as axes and spears, and the controlled use of fire. Either of these species could be the last common ancestor shared by *Homo neanderthalensis* (more commonly known as Neandertals) and *Homo sapiens*, both of whom enter the human fossil record around two hundred thousand years ago.

Neandertals had well-developed brains like us, but they did not think as creatively as we do and their bodies were slightly different. Their heads were larger with heavier brow ridges and a larger nose opening, but not much of a chin. More powerfully built with thicker bones than us, Neandertals had shorter forearms and lower legs. They used advanced tools and left behind indications that they lived in communities that took care of each other. Neandertals primarily inhabited what is now Europe.

Beginning about forty thousand years ago, *Homo sapiens* wandered into Europe from Africa and coexisted with Neandertals until about twenty-seven thousand years ago. For a long time, scientists and the public alike have wondered if humans ever mated with Neandertals and produced children. Don thinks this is unlikely, but recently geneticists from the Max Planck Institute for Evolutionary Anthropology in Germany believe they have found evidence of Neandertal DNA in humans who originated in Europe and the Middle East, outside of Africa. These researchers extracted DNA from Neandertal fossil bones and compared it to human DNA. The tiny amount of Neandertal DNA detected could be explained by mating or it could be insignificant. Even if interbreeding took place on a small scale, it could account for the slight difference in the genetic makeup of today's human beings. In the end, humans may have edged the Neandertal out of existence by competing for the same resources. Whatever caused the extinction of all the other hominins, *Homo sapiens* is the only human species to survive today.

Scientists working in the field are discovering evidence of other extinct *Homo* species around the world. In 2003, a team led by Dr. Michael Morwood found hominin fossils in a cave on the isolated Indonesian island of Flores. These hominins were not much more than three feet tall, like Lucy, but were definitely more humanlike and used simple stone tools. They were given the scientific name *Homo floresiensis* (pronounced floor-ez-ee-EN-sis), and nicknamed "the Hobbit." The species appears to have lived on Flores until seventeen thousand years ago. Some researchers think that ancestors of this species made their way to the island about a million years ago and gradually evolved a shorter stature because of the island's limited resources. Conventional thinking is that *Homo erectus* was the first hominin to leave Africa. *Homo floresiensis* has caused other scientists to wonder if a smaller hominin actually left Africa first to settle in Indonesia.

In 2008, Russian researchers recovered a fossil finger bone from a cave in Siberia. These scientists expected the finger to belong to either *Homo neanderthalensis* or *Homo sapiens.* DNA analysis showed that it was neither. It is possible that another *Homo* species lived at the same time as Neandertals and humans during the last ice age. Scientists will need to find more fossil bones to go with the finger before they can give this species its own name or its own branch on our human family tree.

Homo sapiens

The early *Homo sapiens* (recall, "wise man") branch of the human evolutionary tree distinguished itself from all other hominins by putting its big brain to work to develop technology, language, and culture. Modern human behaviors that evolved thousands of years ago include group cooperation in hunting, creation of more complicated tools, and trade with other groups of people. The ability to think abstractly allowed us to communicate using words and symbols with one another. At least forty thousand years ago (and maybe even earlier), in Africa, our *Homo sapiens* forebears expressed themselves creatively through art. They painted pictures of animals on rocks and cave walls, they carved bones into animal and human shapes, and they decorated their bodies with jewelry made out of animal teeth and shells.

Don is amused that many modern humans think our species is somehow special. Lucy's species lasted some five times as long as we have been around. The evidence is that *Australopithecus afarensis* existed for seven hundred thousand years, while *Homo erectus* was on Earth for over a million years. We modern humans have a long way to go just to match those figures.

Homo sapiens are still undergoing evolutionary processes as our population grows and our environment continues to change, often because of our own actions. Scientists are researching ways that gene mutations might explain the many skin tones and colors we humans possess, the development of disease protection in different groups of people, and the differences in how our bodies process food. We now need to adapt our behaviors for the dramatic climate change we face. Species respond to extreme climate changes by moving to another habitat similar to the previous one, by adapting to the new one, or by going extinct. We cannot wait for the biological changes that take place as mutations in our genes, but we can use our big brains to expand our technologies so we can keep our planet a healthy home where all species, including our own, can thrive.

NOTES

1. Read more about Don and Bill finding an *Australopithecus afarensis* skull in Donald C. Johanson, "Face-to-Face with Lucy's Family," *National Geographic* 189, no. 3 (March 1996): 96–117.

2. Detailed information on Ardi can be found at Jamie Shreeve, "Oldest Skeleton of Human Ancestor Found," *National Geographic* (October 1, 2009), http://news.nationalgeographic.com/news/2009/10/091001-oldest-human-skeleton-ardi-missing-link-chimps-ardipithecus-ramidus.html.

3. To read about the Leakey perspective on the Johanson-Leakey relationship, consult Mary Bowman-Kruhm, *The Leakeys* (Amherst, NY: Prometheus Books, 2010).

4. See Christopher Sloan, "Origin of Childhood," *National Geographic* 210 (November 2006): 148–59, for pictures and an article about the amazing discovery of the Dikika baby.

5. To learn more about the Neandertal controversy, read Kate Wong, "Neandertal Genome Study Reveals That We Have a Little Caveman in Us," *Scientific American* (May 6, 2010), http://www.scientificamerican.com/article.cfm?id=neandertal-genome-study-r.

A convoy of vehicles heading into the desert.
(*Courtesy of the Institute of Human Origins*)

CHAPTER

Six

RISKS, REGRETS, AND REWARDS

When Don is asked about his career, he answers that he has been "lucky." However, a good part of his luck has come about because he has been bold enough to take risks and to take advantage of opportunities for developing and improving the field of paleoanthropology.

Some of the risks Don took as a younger man have already been mentioned—changing his major in college, going to Africa without experience, believing in his abilities as he defended his fossil evidence, naming a new species, and revising the human family tree. In addition to these professional risks, Don had to face physical dangers that made his job as a paleoanthropologist even more challenging.

Scientists who conduct field expeditions in other countries often encounter dangerous working conditions. Many countries in Africa are politically unstable under the control of military governments. Other countries are at war with each other. Ethiopia in the 1970s faced both problems.

After finding Lucy during his 1974 fieldwork, Don took a big risk by returning to Ethiopia in 1975. The political turmoil in the country was even greater than the year before, but Don felt that he and his team would be safe in the remote desert with armed Afar tribesmen watching out for them. Don's reward for taking that risk was finding the First Family.

By 1976, Ethiopia had become so dangerous that the American embassy could not guarantee protection for Don and his field team. But Don considered his research outside the realm of politics and decided to move forward. His reward that year was

Don with his Afar armed guards.
(Courtesy of Nanci Kahn/Institute of Human Origins)

the discovery of stone tools that are probably 2.5 million years old. Shortly after that visit, Ethiopia closed its borders to outside scientists, so the decision to engage in future fieldwork was taken out of Don's hands.

Political problems are not the only dangers facing scientists in the wild: transportation also can be dangerous. Small airplanes and helicopters frequently are used to survey and take photographs of ground features to find the best places to excavate, and these flyovers have provided Don with two close calls. One field season, Don was shooting aerial photographs of a hominin site from a two-seated Cessna plane that was being flown by a bush pilot. As they flew over the crater cap of a volcano, the plane encountered a sudden downdraft and started dropping out of the sky. The pilot had to work quickly to raise the plane, and fortunately he was successful. On another occasion, as Don was flying in a helicopter with former *National Geographic* photographer David Brill to snap aerial photographs of the First Family excavation site, the aircraft lost altitude and ended up crash-landing in the desert. Remarkably, no one on board was seriously injured.

Not all of Don's risky calls took place in the air. During a visit to South Africa while filming a *NOVA* episode, Don was sitting in a Land Rover, watching as a lioness stalked the vehicle. She appeared to consider jumping up on the hood, and Don was struck by the realization that there was no windshield to protect him. He felt vulnerable but managed to remain calm and motionless. The lioness was scared off by the driver, who threw some pebbles across the hood of the vehicle. She walked away, much to Don's great relief.

Scientists have to be prepared to deal with unexpected human behaviors in addition to unpredictable wildlife. In Yemen, located

on the southeastern coast of the Arabian peninsula, Don was sur-
veying for fossil sites with members of his team when a group of
Bedouins with guns stopped their truck and demanded that all the
scientists clear out so they could steal the vehicle. Don knew that
being in the desert without transportation was not a safe option for
his team, so they held their ground and stubbornly refused to
leave the truck. After holding the team hostage for several nerve-
racking hours, the Arab nomads abandoned their efforts to steal
the truck. Don had triumphantly outwaited the would-be
hijackers, and he felt vindicated, if shaken, by his determination.

RISK TAKING

Taking risks is a routine part of human nature. Bravely facing
danger, wisely being open to opportunities, and willingly taking
chances are what leads to new inventions, creative ways of
thinking about things, and a more interesting life. We admire
adventurers who are ready to take risks. And most of us would
not prefer to live completely risk-free because life would be too
boring that way.

Nonetheless, the decision to take a risk must be accompanied
by awareness of possible consequences and the commitment to
be personally responsible for the results of such a decision.
Taking a risk that is too dangerous, intentionally putting oneself
or others in harm's way, or breaking the law is reckless and unrea-
sonable behavior. Some thrill seekers looking for more excitement in their lives take unnecessary and mindless chances. In the
field and in life, risks must be carefully considered ahead of time
to reduce the likelihood of harmful consequences.

As Don has demonstrated, taking risks can be a positive experience. Embracing luck with one's own hands allows a person to follow a dream, pursue a challenge, and make a wonderful life-changing discovery. Yet even a risk taker who believes in his abilities and his quest must be willing to face the possibility of failure while anticipating the probability of success and reward.

> As scientists, our first responsibility is to squeeze the last drop of information out of every bit of evidence we have in hand. But we must also be willing to take the next step, and build from that information theories that will be ready when the next discovery comes along to test their strength. That's what doing science means. Frustrating as it is, the distantly tantalizing truths about our origins will probably not be revealed before we ourselves are buried under the earth. But that will not stop me from testing and retesting new hypotheses, exploring further possibilities. The point is not to be right. The point is to make progress. And you cannot make progress if you are afraid to be wrong.
>
> —DONALD C. JOHANSON, *LUCY'S CHILD*

REGRETS

Over time, Don's willingness to be bold and take risks has cost him certain friendships. He regrets that speaking up for himself to defend his evidence or ambitiously grasping opportunities have pushed some people away from him.

In the field of science, there have been many occasions where scientists who started out as friends and colleagues became bitter enemies because of competition and disagreements. Conflicts have erupted over a fossil's age or significance, over hurt feelings when findings are prematurely announced that take away the attention or publicity from another scientist, or over jealously holding on to new fossils and not sharing them with other researchers.

When Don was a younger man, he was an outspoken scientist. Because he believed so strongly that what he had to say was important, he was not always as careful or as tactful as he should have been. When Don announced the new species *Australopithecus afarensis*, he included some fossil specimens found by Mary Leakey. He thought she would be pleased, and he was surprised to find out how angry she was. Many people, including the Leakeys, believed that Don did not show good manners because he did not consult with and receive Mary's permission first. Now that Don is older, he has mellowed quite a bit and has adopted a more considerate and less confrontational way to express himself. He still feels remorse about lost friendships, and he hopes someday to reconcile with a select few of the people who meant so much to his early career success.

REWARDS

While certain friendships may not have endured, Don believes that he has been fortunate to collaborate with many distinguished and tremendously talented scientists throughout the years. His cooperative work with other paleoanthropologists continues to the present day.

Don's scientific achievements have been recognized many times over in honors and awards. For example, after discovering Lucy and contributing a new view to the field of paleoanthropology, Don was awarded fellowship in the Royal Geographic Society of the United Kingdom. As the society's website shows, membership is "dedicated to the spirit of adventure in the exploration of our world and scientific research to add to the sum of our existing knowledge." Don is in good company along with other famous members, such as the explorers Sir Henry Morton Stanley, Dr. David Livingstone, and Sir Edmund Hillary, as well as the celebrated Charles Darwin.

Among other honors, Don has received recognition for outstanding professional and scientific achievement from the University of Chicago Alumni Association and the American Academy of Achievement. The book he wrote about his discovery, *Lucy: The Beginnings of Humankind*, won a National Book Award for Science in 1982.

Don holds the Virginia M. Ullman Chair in Human Origins at Arizona State University. In the academic world, being awarded an endowed chair is a special honor. Virginia M. Ullman generously donated a large sum of money, called an endowment, to the university to use for funding Don's academic position, as well as several other professorships in the sciences. Funds from the endowment have helped Don to teach, conduct research, and perform his public education service. Recently, Don was recognized for his service as a "tireless public communicator for human evolution" by Case Western Reserve University (CWRU).

Holding the Explorers Club flag in 1990
over the spot where he found Lucy.
(Courtesy of the Institute of Human Origins)

As the Case News Center website reports, Don, a former faculty
member at CWRU, was awarded an honorary doctor of science.

On March 20, 2010, Don received the highest honor a paleoanthropologist can attain. He was awarded the Explorers Medal
for "extraordinary contributions directly in the field of exploration, scientific research, or to the welfare of humanity," as indi-
cated by the Explorers Club website. The Explorers Club pro-
motes scientific exploration and field research of land, sea, air,
and space. Since 1904, their flag has been carried on hundreds of

expeditions in each of those environments. Don joined the ranks of such distinguished medalists as Admiral Robert Edwin Peary, astronaut Neil Armstrong, Thor Heyerdahl, Jane Goodall, and the Leakey family.

There are particular awards that have sentimental meaning for Don. He is proud that the American Anthropological Association recognized him for his work in popularizing science for the general public. Don also is fond of his honor from the Academy of Sciences in Siena because of his connection to Italy, one of his favorite vacation destinations. Perhaps Don's greatest reward for taking so many risks to become a respected scientist is the vast network of friends, fellow scientists, and interested persons throughout the world who have learned more about their human origins as a result of his work.

Don presenting Lucy to other scientists at the
Nobel symposium in Karlskoga, Sweden, in 1978.
(Courtesy of John Reader)

CHAPTER Seven

DON'S LEGACY

In order to move forward as a species, we need to embrace our past and understand our place in nature.

—DONALD C. JOHANSON

BEING A PALEOANTHROPOLOGIST

When Don started his career, he expected that he would be primarily a college professor someday. But then, at age thirty-one, his achievements made him famous and redirected his life plans. Some people have a hard time dealing with attaining fame early in life. They reach the pinnacle of their sport or career when young, and nothing ever again matches their early success. Others, like Don, handle youthful accomplishment with a maturity that enables them to adjust and to create a lasting body of work built upon a successful foundation.

The discovery of Lucy and other fossils elevated Don to the

status of one of the world's leading scientists. Being a paleoanthropologist is not just about finding old bones. Also, it is about
being a diplomat, learning to disagree with others in a respectful
manner and accepting criticism or praise with an open mind.
That includes serving as a spokesperson for science and teaching
both future scientists and the general public to be excited about
what has yet to be discovered and where science may still lead us.

Don was not prepared as a public speaker, but he quickly
learned to be an effective communicator so he could easily share
information about Lucy with other scientists. At the same time,
the public became fascinated by Lucy and wanted to know more
about our human origins. Don soon discovered his hidden talent
for relating science to people in a way they could understand.

Don began to give lectures to the public, write popular books,
and narrate documentaries for public television. He was criticized by some scientists for getting too far away from the actual
work of science. Believing that no one owns knowledge and that
science should not be kept a secret, Don felt a duty to enlighten
people about how we came to be human. Don still travels around
the world, speaking to groups of people. He has presented in a
variety of formats: from a grand Nobel symposium in Karlskoga,
Sweden, the country of his parents' birth; through IMAX the-
aters in science museums; to humble school gymnasiums.

In 1978, the Royal Swedish Academy of Sciences invited Don
to give a presentation on the hominins he had found at Hadar.
This was several years after Don had discovered Lucy and the
First Family but before he had introduced them to the world.
Don thought that a Nobel symposium would be a good place to
reveal a new species. Many scientists present were shocked at this
young scientist's audacity, but Don bravely stood his ground.

Many laypeople are also shocked by what Don has to say about evolution, so Don often begins his public talks by comparing the acceptance of the theory of evolution to the acceptance of the theory of gravity. The theory of evolution is not an attack on religion any more than gravity is. Science explains the existence of both evolution and gravity. It is up to philosophy and religion to help people figure out what is right or wrong behavior. The fact of evolution does not take away from any individual's private beliefs or faith. While some people choose to believe that humans were created as we are now, Don's search for human ancestors has convinced him that we were not created separately. Humans are a part of nature, and we are connected to, and we evolved along with, all life on the planet.

Don urges that general evolution be introduced to students in elementary school. He would like to see schoolchildren learn why life on Earth is so diverse. He especially would like children to understand that because we hold a place in the natural world, we have an impact on nature—we interact with it—and for that reason, how our actions change nature can come back to have an effect on us later. By high school, children should be taught human evolution, allowing them to marvel at how we came to be what we are. That approach may inspire some of them to study science and biology in college.

Recently, in his books and in his talks, Don has been a more outspoken advocate for protecting the environment. Because we are a part of nature, we need to be more responsible about using our world's resources. Our species must stop being so wasteful and destructive and try to fit in better with the natural flow of Earth. We also must stop cutting down forests that reduce habitats and threaten extinction of our nearest primate relatives. Don thinks it should be a human priority to save the chimpanzees, bonobos, gorillas, and orangutans with which we share a common ancestor that goes back before even Lucy's time.

DON'S WRITINGS AND COMMUNICATIONS

Lucy: The Beginnings of Humankind (with Maitland Edey), 1981

Lucy's Child: The Discovery of a Human Ancestor (with James Shreeve), 1989

Blueprints: Solving the Mystery of Evolution (with Maitland Edey), 1989

Journey from the Dawn: Life with the World's First Family (with Kevin O'Farrell), 1990

Ancestors: In Search of Human Origins (with Lenora Johanson and Blake Edgar), 1994

From Lucy to Language (with Blake Edgar), 1996

Lucy's Legacy: The Quest for Human Origins (with Kate Wong), 2009

PBS *NOVA* three-part series, *In Search of Human Origins*, original broadcast in 1994

Institute of Human Origins websites: http://iho.asu.edu/ and http://www.becominghuman.org/

INSTITUTE OF HUMAN ORIGINS

After finding Lucy and the First Family, Don continued to make important contributions to the field of paleoanthropology. His professional dream had been to create a research facility devoted to the study of human prehistory. In 1981, Don left Cleveland, Ohio, to establish the Institute of Human Origins (IHO) in Berkeley, California. Don's main goal was to bring together scientists with a variety of backgrounds from around the world. He envisioned geologists, archeologists, biologists, and primatologists (scientists who study apes) combining their efforts with paleoanthropologists to study and understand new discoveries. He also intended to train students, both American and foreign, to conduct research expanding the science's knowledge base; to financially support field expeditions and lab work; and to provide science education to the general public. By 1997, IHO had expanded and moved to Tempe, Arizona, to partner with Arizona State University, where it continues to move science forward today.

In 2008, Don reached the age of sixty-five and decided to pass along some of his administrative responsibilities at IHO. Don relishes his new role as the founding director of the institute because it keeps him involved in IHO's work. Don is particularly gifted at raising money to fund research and fieldwork. Grants from the National Science Foundation and the National Geographic Society, though generous, do not cover all the institute's expenses. So Don raises necessary operating funds from private corporations and individuals through his many speaking engagements.

Don's former student, good friend, and respected colleague, Bill Kimbel, is the new director of IHO. Bill is the studious academic Don imagined he was going to be. Bill plans to continue with Don's original goals for the institute, with a strategic plan for the future expanding of IHO's prominence internationally. Bill foresees IHO scientists collaborating more globally with scientists at other institutions around the world. He also predicts that paleoanthropology will incorporate a more collaborative and diversified approach to the study of hominin fossil remains. For example, beyond studying the bones separately, scientists are investigating how early humans developed in their parts of the world, in particular, how they responded to changes in climate and challenges in their ancient environments. Furthermore, IHO scientists are examining evidence of migrations and extinctions among the variety of species that preceded *Homo sapiens*. IHO is definitely in able hands with plenty of important work left to do.

THE MAN HIMSELF

With his deep, resonating voice and professorial manner, Don can seem intimidating at first. But his off-kilter smile and the twinkle in his eye reveal a quick-witted joke teller with a mischievous sense of humor. Don's humor, when combined with a self-confidence derived from his vast knowledge, makes him a terrific public speaker. Another factor that makes Don a successful communicator is his skill with languages. He speaks passable Italian, French, German, and Swedish. Along his travels, Don has picked up some Amharic, the language of Ethiopia, and enough words in other African languages to get by in those countries.

Don admits that he has been overly dedicated to his career to the point that his heavy workload and being away on field expeditions interfered with maintaining personal relationships. He is currently single after having been married three times. With his third wife, Lenora, Don adopted an Ethiopian boy named Tesfaye (Amharic for "my hope"). Don's son is now a young man living in California.

Life cannot be all work and no play. When Don was a teenager, his mother presented him with his late father's camera. Don taught himself photography, and it is still one of his favorite hobbies. Don enjoys taking photographs of people, wildlife, and

Don showing his cameras to Afar children.
(Used by permission of David Brill)

Don as a wildlife photographer in Madagascar, 2008.
(Photograph by CAP Saucier)

landscapes as he travels around the world. Many of his best shots have been published in his books, in IHO brochures, and in museum displays.

Don is an elegant and well-dressed man. His other diversions include a taste for fine wine and fine art. Don's art collection represents a range from Renaissance-era Albrecht Durer engravings and a Tiepolo watercolor to recently acquired contemporary African art. He also entertains himself by playing golf occasionally.

Don was not raised in a religious household and is not affiliated with a particular religion. Still, in recent years, Don has become a student of Buddhism. He takes pleasure in studying a philosophy of mindfulness, and learning to live in the present moment has helped him be a calmer person. Don especially likes that Buddhism emphasizes kindness and compassion toward all other living beings.

Opera Aficionado

Don developed a passion for opera as a child, and it has continued throughout his life. So what is opera? Opera is a combination of theater and music that tells a story. It is not just for older rich people; it is for people who have experienced enough of life and love to appreciate the drama unfolding on stage. Opera offers a variety of timeless tales of love, jealousy, revenge, courage, and sadness sung with powerful voices. It is usually set in historic times and in other countries, and it is often performed in languages such as Italian and German (but with English subtitles, as in foreign films). Opera presents people dealing with great emotions that are too strong for mere words. Dramatic music adds force to the emotions.

Don can temporarily get away from thinking about his work by listening to or viewing live opera. One of Don's dreams came true not long ago when he performed as a cast member, first in *La Boheme* and then in *Aida*, for the Phoenix Opera Company. Don's favorite opera is *The Ring of Nibelungen*, by Richard Wagner. This piece is actually a cycle of four operas depicting the struggles of gods and goddesses over a magic ring that gives power over the world. It is a dramatic tale of love, betrayal, and the corrupting influence of power.

Reflection

When Don looks back on his career, he identifies his early professional years as his happiest. The 1970s were a time when the science of paleoanthropology came into its own and began to grow. Fresh out of graduate school with few worries or responsibilities, Don was excited to be a part of a budding science. It was a time of thrilling new discoveries that captured the public's imagination.

Don wants to be remembered as a trailblazer in the science of evolution. He is often recognized in public because he still makes appearances on television to give his opinion whenever a new discovery is announced. People do not always know his name and sometimes call him "The Lucy Man." So he will always be known as the scientist who discovered Lucy, but to Don, the significance of finding the first hominin in Hadar is that it led to more exceptional discoveries and a deeper understanding of human origins.

Ethiopia is planning to build a museum to house its abundance of hominin fossils about an hour away from where Lucy was found. Don traveled to Ethiopia to help secure a grant from the National Geographic Society and to offer suggestions for designing the exhibits. Don still feels a sense of adventure and connection when he returns to Ethiopia. He likes to remind people in his talks that "we are all Africans."

Don's greatest legacy will likely be his inspiration to future generations of scientists. Don has been bold and passionate in his approach to science, and he has been able to motivate young people to undertake science in the same way. In high school, Don read about Mary and Louis Leakey finding *Zinjanthropus boisei*

(Zinj, now known as *Australopithecus boisei*) in the *New York Times*. Don's enthusiasm to search for fossils and learn about human origins was fired up by this article. Several graduating classes of college students have followed similarly in his footsteps after reading *Lucy: The Beginnings of Humankind.*

It is important to Don that he be thought of as an accessible resource to people. His mentor, Dr. Clark Howell, was a cordial and approachable man who welcomed a young, inexperienced student into his program. Don strives to treat students in the same manner. He tries to personally answer all the letters and e-mails he receives, especially those from schoolchildren.

Don working in the field lab of the Lucy Club.
(Courtesy of the Institute of Human Origins)

CHAPTER
Eight
THE FUTURE OF HUMAN PREHISTORY

There will always be more to learn in our quest for understanding of mankind's origins.

—DONALD C. JOHANSON

After reading about Don's amazing discoveries, one might think there are no more exciting finds to make. In fact, new fossils that present science with more questions in need of answers continue to be uncovered. Site 333, where the First Family was found, still reveals new fossils. From the original two hundred pieces, there are now more than three hundred, and the group of thirteen individuals has grown to eighteen. Not only are there new fossil finds to study, but as the technology of analyzing fossils advances, the older fossils, such as Lucy and the First Family, still need to be scrutinized to learn even more about them.

New technologies are being developed that better determine the age of rocks and fossils. The genetic work of molecular biologists is more accurately predicting when humans last shared a common ancestor with apes. Because humans have so many genes in common with today's apes, genetics also is investigating how those genes are alike or different in order to better understand our collective past.

While Don appreciates advances in scientific technology, he is concerned that humans are becoming so dependent on technology that we are losing our connection to the natural world. We have created an artificial world with our machines—a world that is causing us to be less active and to care less about our impact on nature. Lucy and other early humans were physically active, and we should reclaim that part of our heritage and spend more time outside exercising. Strengthening our connection to nature would result in humanity seeking to preserve the health of our planet. Don wants people to realize that extinction is a common result of evolution. If we do not take care of ourselves and our environment, extinction is a definite possibility. Don would like humans to leave descendants who will look back and wonder about us.

FOSSIL GAPS

Paleoanthropology has amassed a great deal of information about *Australopithecus afarensis*, thanks to Lucy and the First Family. But what existed before Lucy? And who was the first human? Scientists have identified two major gaps in the fossil record that need exploration to answer these questions.

The first gap occurs between six and four million years ago, the estimated time when human ancestors diverged from the ancestors of chimpanzees. A handful of hominin fossils indicate that our ancestors began to walk upright around that time, but the condition of the fossils is too poor to tell much more about what caused humans and apes to evolve in different directions.

To fill this gap, Don recommends that his fellow paleoanthropologists explore other parts of Africa, in addition to Ethiopia and Kenya. They might find older rock deposits from seven to five million years of age that hold fossils of the same age. Unfortunately, there are many land and political barriers to overcome in Africa that prevent scientists from digging so deep into our past. The first hominin to walk upright could be buried under a layer of rock formed by the lava flow of an ancient volcano in an area researchers cannot yet access.

The second fossil gap has been identified between three and two million years ago. There are very few fossils to show the link between the australopithecines and *Homo*, when the hominin brain began enlarging and when tool making emerged.

In 1996, two Afar workers under the supervision of IHO director Bill Kimbel discovered an upper jaw in Hadar, Ethiopia. Dated at 2.3 million years of age, the jaw belonged to a creature with a shorter face than an australopithecine but with larger and more primitive teeth than *Homo habilis*, currently the first *Homo* on our family tree. Scientists speculate that the jaw is evidence of an unknown *Homo* species that could actually represent the first human to evolve. Only more fossils of that age with different body parts will tell us for sure.

Both Don and Bill agree that hunting for fossils is an exciting part of being a paleoanthropologist. Not every paleoanthropologist will be so fortunate as to make a major discovery. There are plenty of fossils already found for future scientists to study, analyze, and interpret their significance. Learning as much as we can

Don with the actual Lucy fossil in Discovery Times Square, New York City, 2009. *(Used by permission of Chester Higgins Jr./ The New York Times/Redux)*

about each fossil will make a contribution to the field of paleo-anthropology. The professor in Bill would like to see students who are curious, creative, and clever thinkers enter the field. He looks forward to teaching students who can devise new ways of analyzing information, express new ways of thinking about what we already know, and energize science with questions that have not yet been asked.

If the science of paleoanthropology were a book, it would read like a great mystery novel. The main character of the book has a wealth of fossil clues and questions to answer, such as "Whose jaw is this?" There is a fascinating cast of personalities, scientists past and present, in competition and conflict with one another. Will the ultimate goal of the profession, to find a unified theory of human evolution, be accomplished?

A reader learning about human origins will want to turn each page to learn more about it. The end of the story of human origins has not been yet written because of the work still to be done. There are many mysteries left to solve, and they will be answered by tomorrow's restless young scientists who are driven by a sense of wonder and adventure.

Don considers himself a lucky man, but we are the lucky ones to benefit from his intense dedication to science. Let us hope that those following in his footsteps exhibit the courage and intelligence that contributed to Don's successful and productive career as a respected paleoanthropologist.

ACKNOWLEDGMENTS

Writing a book is a particularly solitary activity, but it requires the loyal assistance of many people. I would like to thank my husband, Pete, and daughter, Megan Molitoris, for their encouragement and for reading every word of my manuscript, from rough draft to final copy. Thanks also to my daughters, Joanne and Valerie Saucier, for their love and support. I appreciate the role my dear friend Frank Kollman assumed as Photoshop guru to help me produce wonderful photographs. My favorite fifth-grade teacher, Jamie Nicholson, contributed to the book by making sure my vocabulary level was appropriate for young readers. Many thanks go to the staff of the Institute of Human Origins, especially Bethany Baker and Cara Lancellotti for helping me sort through and select photographs from their extensive archives.

I am grateful to my new friend and fellow writer, Mary Bowman-Kruhm, for introducing me to Prometheus Books. A special thanks is extended to my editor, Steven L. Mitchell, for taking a chance on a rookie writer.

To Bill Kimbel, my friend and IHO director, I want to express my appreciation for the time he provided me to answer questions, define terms, and share his knowledge. Finally, but most important, I thank my good friend, Don Johanson, for his patience and generosity during interviews, manuscript proofreading, and photograph selection. Don has enriched my life as he has educated me to the wonders of our human origins, introduced me to fascinating people, and guided me to astonishing places in the world, such as the painted caves of southern France and the rain forests of Madagascar.

A portion of the proceeds from this book will be donated to Ethiopia Reads, a nonprofit organization that opens school libraries for and provides books to the children of Ethiopia (http://www.ethiopiareads.org/). I thank the archives of the Cleveland Museum of Natural History and Case Western Reserve University for each contributing a photograph to this project. Besides Don and Bill, the following talented photographers donated their photographs in support of this cause: Lenora Carey, Enrico Ferorelli, and Nanci Kahn.

BIBLIOGRAPHY

BOOKS

Bergquist, James M. *Daily Life in Immigrant America, 1820–1870.* Chicago: Ivan R. Dee, 2009.

Bowman-Kruhm, Mary. *The Leakeys.* Amherst, NY: Prometheus Books, 2010.

Bradley, James V. *How Species Change.* New York: Infobase, 2006.

Cronkite, Walter. *A Reporter's Life.* New York: Alfred A. Knopf, 2008.

Gish, Steven, Winnie Thay, Zawiah Abdul Latif. *Ethiopia.* New York: Marshall Cavendish Benchmark, 2007.

Hall, John G. *Ethiopia in the Modern World.* Philadelphia: Chelsea House, 2003.

Heinrichs, Ann. *Ethiopia.* New York: Children's Press, 2005.

Huxley, Thomas H. *Man's Place in Nature.* Mineola, NY: Dover, 2003. Originally published New York: D. Appleton, 1863.

Johanson, Donald C., and Blake Edgar. *From Lucy to Language.* 2nd ed. New York: Simon & Schuster, 2006.

Johanson, Donald C., and James Shreeve. *Lucy's Child: The Discovery of a Human Ancestor.* New York: William Morrow, 1989.

Johanson, Donald C., and Kate Wong. *Lucy's Legacy.* New York: Harmony Books, 2009.

Johanson, Donald C., and Kevin O'Farrell. *Journey from the Dawn.* New York: Villard Books, 1990.

Johanson, Donald C., Lenora Johanson, and Blake Edgar. *Ancestors: The Search for Our Human Origins.* New York: Villard Books, 1994.

Johanson, Donald C., and Maitland Edey. *Lucy: The Beginnings of Humankind.* New York: Simon & Schuster, 1981.

———. *Blueprints: Solving the Mystery of Evolution.* Boston: Little, Brown, 1989.

Lockwood, Charles. *The Human Story.* London: Natural History Museum, 2007.

Powell, John. *Encyclopedia of North American Immigration.* New York: Facts on File, 2005.

Sadie, Stanley, ed. *The Billboard Illustrated Encyclopedia of Opera.* New York: Watson-Guptill, 2004.

Sloan, Christopher. *The Human Story.* Washington, DC: National Geographic Society, 2004.

Tattersall, Ian. *The World from Beginnings to 4000 BCE.* New York: Oxford University Press, 2008.

Wilson, Edward O., ed. *From So Simple a Beginning: The Four Great Books of Charles Darwin.* New York: W. W. Norton, 2006.

ARTICLES

Case Western Reserve University News Center. "Case Western Reserve University to Award Honorary Degrees." May 14, 2009. http://blog.case.edu/case-news/2009/05/14/honorarydegrees 2009.

Dalton, Rex. "Fossil Finger Points to New Human Species." *Nature* 464 (March 25, 2010): 472–73.

Johanson, Donald C. "Ethiopia Yields First 'Family' of Early Man." *National Geographic* 150, no. 6 (December 1976): 790–811.

———. "Face-to-Face with Lucy's Family. *National Geographic* 189, no. 3 (March 1996): 96–117.

Shreeve, Jamie. "Oldest Skeleton of Human Ancestor Found." *National Geographic* (October 1, 2009), http://news.nationalgeographic.com/news/2009/10/091001-oldest-human-skeleton-ardi-missing-link-chimps-ardipithecus-ramidus.html.

Sloan, Christopher. "Origin of Childhood." *National Geographic* 210 (November 2006): 148–59.

Smith, Langdon. *Evolution: A Fantasy.* Boston: J. W. Luce, 1909.

Weaver, Kenneth F. "Stones, Bones, and Early Man: The Search for Our Ancestors." *National Geographic* 168, no. 5 (November 1985): 560–623.

Wong, Kate. "Neandertal Genome Study Reveals That We Have a Little Caveman in Us." *Scientific American* (May 6, 2010), http://www.scientificamerican.com/article.cfm?id=neandertal-genome-study-r.

———. "Spectacular South African Skeletons Reveal New Species from Murky Period of Human Evolution." *Scientific American* (April 8, 2010), http://www.scientificamerican.com/article.cfm?id=south-african-hominin-fossil.

WEBSITES

American Museum of Natural History, Hall of Human Origins, http://www.amnh.org/exhibitions/permanent/humanorigins/

The Explorers Club, http://www.explorers.org/

Institute of Human Origins, http://iho.asu.edu/ and http://www.becominghuman.org/

Royal Geographic Society of the United Kingdom, http://www.rgs.org/

Smithsonian National Museum of Natural History, http://humanorigins.si.edu/

INDEX

Page numbers in **boldface** refer to photographs and illustrations.